Thinning the Herd

Thinning the Herd

Tales of the Weirdly Departed

CYNTHIA CEILÁN

THE LYONS PRESS
Guilford, Connecticut
AN IMPRINT OF THE GLOBE PEQUOT PRESS

The Lyons Press is an imprint of The Globe Pequot Press.

10 9 8 7 6 5 4 3 2 1

Printed in the United States of America
DESIGNED BY CLAIRE ZOGHB

ISBN 978-1-59921-219-7

Library of Congress Cataloging-in-Publication Data

Ceilán, Cynthia.
  Thinning the herd : tales of the weirdly departed / Cynthia Ceilán.
      p. cm.
  Includes bibliographical references.
  ISBN-13: 978-1-59921-219-7
  1. Biography–Anecdotes. 2. Death–Anecdotes. 3. Curiosities and wonders. I. Title.
  CT105.C29 2007
  920.02--dc22

                                  2007034168

For **Mike** and **Jeff**

Table of Contents

Acknowledgments

Thank you, Holly Rubino of The Lyons Press, for letting your inner ghoul come out and play.

Thank you, Mom, for not sending the police after me, like you promised, when I ran away to college.

Thank you, Dad, for the gift of laughter, and for being there, no matter what.

Thank you, Mike and Jeff, for being my little brothers. I have observed your weirdness from up close for many years. You, more than anyone else in the world, make me feel normal.

And thank you, Christopher, for your support, your encouragement, your love, and—most especially—for being careful not to step on Pee-Pee Petie.

Introduction

I WANT TO DIE IN MY SLEEP LIKE MY GRANDFATHER, NOT
YELLING AND SCREAMING LIKE THE PASSENGERS IN HIS CAR.

—Will Shriner

THOSE OF US who embrace a certain fascination with particularly
odd ways of dying tend to shrug off suggestions that we might
be a little bit nuts. Deep down, however, we fear our friends and
loved ones may be right. We nevertheless find solace, and perhaps
even a little pride, in knowing that we manage to live and work
among the normal people, very often undetected. We have families, jobs, mortgages, and, occasionally, we serve on juries.

Death, to most of us, is the sort of thing that only happens
to other people, namely the very dumb, the very crazy, and the
very unlucky. We, of course, are not other people. We are smart,
and we are sane. We are going to live forever. And then one day,
when we are 117 years old, we will go to sleep for a long, long
time, and when we wake up, the icky part will be over.

Everybody else we call crazy: our beloved agoraphobics, the panic-stricken, the hypochondriacs, the under-medicated, the inexplicably enraged, and those guys who wear tinfoil on their heads to deflect alien death rays.

But think about this for a moment. Aren't these, in fact, the people who know better than anyone else that they are *not* likely to die of old age in their sleep?

So who's crazy?

Not all deaths are funny, of course. Some are sad. Some are spooky. And some serve to reassure us that we do, indeed, live in a just universe. Death can be fair in ways that life too often is not.

Me? I hope I go laughing.

Cynthia Ceilán
New York City
April 2007

1

OOPS

IF ALL ELSE FAILS, IMMORTALITY CAN ALWAYS BE
ASSURED BY SPECTACULAR ERROR.
—John Kenneth Galbraith (1908–2006)

I WONDER HOW often, in the normal course of any ordinary day, each of us comes this close to meeting the Reaper without ever realizing it.

As human beings, we've probably evolved ourselves right out of whatever natural ability or animal instinct we may have once possessed that warned us of approaching danger before we saw it, smelled it, or heard it coming. I understand that farm animals and pets get really weird long before a natural disaster actually strikes, as in the case of earthquakes and tornadoes. I, on the other hand, once slept right through a horrendous storm, gale force winds and all, only to wake up the following morning to find that my neighbor's 30-foot tree had been ripped out of his front yard and thrown onto the roof of my house. "Wow," I thought, when I saw that a good portion of the tree had landed directly above my bedroom, "this could have been bad."

How often have I pushed my way past the wrong stranger on a crowded New York City subway platform, someone who was almost crazy enough to shove me right onto the train tracks just to teach me a lesson in civility? Or found myself barreling down the highway in a near state of hypnosis with Bob Seger's "Hollywood Nights" blaring from the speakers full blast, and realizing I had just changed lanes without checking my blind spot? Or mistakenly unplugged the coffeemaker instead of the toaster before sticking a fork into it to retrieve my English muffin?

I'm sure I've been lucky more often than I will ever know. The same is probably true for most people. For others, not so much.

Thinning the Herd

John Lewis of Minsterworth, England, set out to do a little gardening one fine day in the summer of 1999. He snipped some shrubs, weeded his garden, and raked up the debris into an average-sized pile. He poured some gasoline over it to get a good bonfire going, then lit a match. The ensuing explosion engulfed most of John's clothing in flames, but he was able to run toward a nearby river to put himself out. Unfortunately, he couldn't swim. John drowned and was dragged several miles downstream. His body was found two weeks later, clad only in socks and shoes.

Among other things, American playwright Tennessee Williams was rather fond of his nasal spray. While staying in a New York City hotel in 1983, he choked to death on the bottle cap, which had fallen from his hand into his mouth while he was taking a snort.

Nazari Omar Baki was a seasoned Malaysian movie stuntman. While shooting a scene in the 2007 movie *Jangan Pandang Belakang,* in which a ghost was chasing him, Omar leapt from the fourth floor of a building, completely missing the stack of mattresses below. He died on impact.

Before the invention of anesthesia, speed was of the essence in performing surgery. Dr. Robert Liston (1794–1847) was arguably the fastest scalpel on record. He is reputed to have been able to amputate and suture a limb in thirty seconds flat. Unfortunately, accuracy was not as big a priority for the good doctor. He once amputated a man's leg—and his testicles—in a single swipe of the knife.

Liston's most infamous claim to fame, however, is being the only surgeon on record to have a 300 percent mortality rate during a single operation. He accidentally cut off the fingers of his surgical assistant, who later died of septic shock. Liston also slashed through the coattails of a colleague observing the operation, who died of fright on the spot, thinking that Liston had severed his vital organs. The patient survived the procedure, but later died of gangrene.

While on board the RMS *Queen Mary* in 1949, 2nd Officer William Stark decided to take a wee nip from the captain's secret stash of liquor. As Stark would find out a bit too late, the captain used his old gin bottles to store tetrachloride, an effective yet highly poisonous cleaning solvent.

Seeking relief for her neck and back problems, Lana Dale Lewis of Toronto went to her chiropractor for a routine adjustment in September 1996. She suffered a series of strokes after getting her neck "cracked." The last stroke proved fatal.

The clown act of Jo-Jo and Mr. Ollie was pretty standard circus fare in the early 1900s. A big mean guy (Jo-Jo) terrorizes a hapless little guy (Mr. Ollie).

In real life, Jo-Jo and Ollie were good friends. They were also avid drinking buddies. One night, after a few too many preshow tipples, Jo-Jo forgot to put on his wooden wig. At the climax of the act, when Mr. Ollie bests his nemesis by hitting him on the head with a hatchet, Jo-Jo fell dead on the sawdust for real.

Circus clowns immediately descended on the scene from all corners of the tent to carry Jo-Jo out on a stretcher before anyone in the audience could realize the performers' tragic error. Unfortunately, they grabbed a prop stretcher by mistake. When they lifted the poles and ran, Jo-Jo stayed behind on the ground, still gushing blood from his head, still dead.

A distraught Mr. Ollie ran around the center ring of the big top, crying and screaming, and tripped over his own big floppy shoes. He suffered only minor injuries in the fall.

The secret code for prompting the circus ushers to clear the tent during an emergency called for the band to play "Stars and Stripes Forever." Instead, they played "Strike Up the Band." Everyone rose to their feet, cheering maniacally.

It was far and away the greatest moment in the history of Jo-Jo and Mr. Ollie's clowning career.

An unidentified young man from the port city of Haiphong found an interesting-looking tennis ball in a ditch one day in 2002. When he used it to play a game of catch with some friends, the ball exploded, killing him and injuring six others. The tennis ball turned out to be a small American bomb left over from the Vietnam War.

Sixteen-year-old Li Xiao Meng of China dreamed of being a rock star. While playing his air guitar and bouncing up and down on his bed, he accidentally flew out his third-story bedroom window. He did not survive the fall.

In 2006, Sharffe Williams from Oakland, California, was caught on videotape robbing a liquor store. He almost got away with it, too. When he put his gun back into the waistband of his pants, he accidentally shot himself in the leg. Police found his body at the end of a trail of blood, not far from the scene of the robbery.

Jean-Baptiste Lully was an impassioned seventeenth-century composer and conductor. He got a little carried away one day while conducting a religious concert. Lully stabbed himself in the foot with his baton, which at the time was more like a staff, and later died of gangrene.

François Faber of Luxembourg and Hugh Munro of England had a lot in common, though there is no indication that they ever knew each other personally. Faber became famous as a Tour de France winner; Munro became famous writing novels under the name Saki. Both fought in World War I, both died in battle, and both were killed by German snipers. Most remarkably, both made the same stupid mistake. Faber received a telegram in 1915, informing him that his wife had given birth to a baby girl. Elated, he jumped up and cheered, and was promptly shot. About a year later, in another ditch far, far away, Munro stood up and yelled at one of his fellow officers, "Put that damned cigarette out!" Ditto.

On Election Day, 2006, Sam Duncan handily won his bid for a county board seat in Monroe, North Carolina, despite one minor flaw: He had been dead for more than a month. Election officials knew Duncan was dead, but didn't tell the voters. "We are instructed that it's not our job to do that," explained elections director Shirley Secrest.

Péter Vályi, the finance minister of Hungary, knew pretty much nothing about the production of steel. Nevertheless, he visited a steelworks factory in 1973 and performed an inspection that was largely ceremonial. When he stepped up to get a better look at a blast furnace, he fell right in.

By most accounts, French composer Charles-Valentin Alkan (1813–1888) was a man of great faith. To prove it, he wrote phenomenally difficult piano pieces. While reaching for a volume near the top of his bookcase, he lost his balance, which caused the bookcase to topple over on top of him. He survived the fall, but was killed by the avalanche of books.

Director Boris Sagal was so immersed in his work during the filming of the 1982 television miniseries *World War III* that he didn't notice how close he was to danger. He was walking backward while explaining his vision of one particular scene and stepped directly into the path of a spinning helicopter rotor blade. He was hacked to pieces.

Matthew Miller, a farmer from Minnesota, became one with his work when he got caught in his own hay baler. A relative was with him at the time the accident occurred. She said she was pretty sure Miller was dead before he knew what had happened to him.

In November 2006, a woman named Selvaradha from Vasanthanagar, India, caught fire while cooking dinner. Her husband,

Natrayan, immediately stepped in and began beating the flames consuming his wife's sari. He, too, perished in the blaze.

☙

If Guinness had a record for the world's most accident-prone people, Frances and Michael Mosey of Scotland would surely be strong contenders for the title. Frances's run of bad luck began at the age of 5, when she fell from a table and shot a bamboo cane through the roof of her mouth. Other accidents in Frances's astonishingly long life include crashing her bike into a concrete lamppost, getting her legs trapped in the back of her father's tractor, falling into a 6-foot pothole and breaking both legs, breaking a toe when she dropped a sewing machine on it, fracturing her skull when a hospital ceiling tile fell on her head while she was recovering from a hernia operation, fracturing an ankle while buying ice cream for her granddaughter, and slicing off a finger—which her dog promptly ate.

Until Michael Mosey met Frances, he had led a pretty normal life. Afterward, things changed. Over the years, Michael fell through a greenhouse—on three separate occasions. He also cut his forehead on a glass coffee table, fell off a chair and broke his back, broke his right leg after accidentally standing on a puppy, was partially blinded after drinking a bottle of tainted black-market vodka, and got run over by a car while riding home on his new motorcycle.

The driver of the car that hit him was, of course, his wife, Frances.

Left to his own devices, Michael might have lived to recover from many more accidents. Sadly, his streak was broken in 2003 when, at the age of 57, an intruder broke into his home and beat him to death.

One of the reasons why teenagers are considered a high-risk group is that it is often very difficult to convince them that warning signs are rarely posted for decorative purposes only. Loitering under one such sign outside a state-run oil company in Jakarta in 2006, three young people identified as Okri Susilo, Harianto, and Marianto blew themselves up when one of them made a call on his cell phone. The sign warned that the radio emissions from a cell phone could spark an explosion in the giant tanks filled with highly flammable gas. The sign, though futile in this instance, was absolutely correct.

In June 1988, a Ukrainian man died after consuming tainted liquor he had obtained on the black market. At his funeral, ten of his mourners also died. They had each taken a drink from the same supply of alcohol.

In 1991, the small Piper Aerostar plane carrying Pennsylvania senator John Heinz and six others was experiencing problems with its landing gear. A helicopter was sent up to check it out and provide assistance. The chopper collided with the plane, killing everyone on board, as well as a few people on the ground.

Ormer Locklear was an actor and fearless stunt pilot in the early days of flight and moviemaking. He once calmly walked onto his aircraft while in mid-flight to plug a rag into the opening of the radiator when the cap blew off. While filming a night scene in the 1920 silent movie *The Skywayman*, he crash-landed into a group of oil rigs parked at DeMille Airfield in California. The movie crew had forgotten to turn on the runway lights.

Dag Hammarskjöld, the UN secretary general, was on a plane with fifteen others in 1961. They were on their way to a peace mission in the Congo. While flying over Zambia (formerly Rhodesia), someone on the ground fired a warning shot to alert the pilot of a pos-

Thinning the Herd

sible attack by Katanga rebels. The bullet hit the plane, causing it
to crash in the jungle.

Daniel Wright of Gary, Indiana, donned a bulletproof vest and asked
a friend to shoot him with a .20-gauge shotgun. The vest turned
out to be a flak jacket, not a projectile repellent.

Nguyen Van Hung of Cambodia was known to millions as the amaz-
ing "Hung Electric." Hung appeared on numerous television pro-
grams demonstrating his ability to withstand high-voltage electric
shocks. He died in his home in 2006 when he forgot to turn off the
power before repairing a generator.

After not hearing from Marina Weber for several days, her family reported the petite 38-year-old woman missing. Eleven days after
filing the missing persons report, Marina's mother and sister noticed a strange odor in the house. Following their noses, they found

Marina wedged behind a 6-foot bookcase. She had fallen headfirst and become trapped behind the bookcase when she tried to adjust her television set, which sat on the top shelf.

A homeless man from New York found a manhole in Brooklyn that was just out of the way enough to offer him some privacy, so he routinely used it as his toilet. He lost his balance one day and was found dead at the bottom of the sewer.

Marie Rose's husband became alarmed when he woke up one morning in 2006 and could not find his wife. Police arrived to find that the Roses had filled nearly every inch of their Shelton, Washington, home from floor to ceiling with stacks of clothing, dishes, boxes, newspapers, books, and miscellaneous debris. After a ten-hour search, officers finally found Marie buried under an enormous pile of trash, with a telephone in her hand. Mr. Rose was then able to piece together what had probably happened: Marie had a number of health problems, and was very likely trying to call for help when one of the mountains of garbage collapsed on her.

John J. Taylor of Wisconsin considered himself a very lucky man. While serving in the army during World War II, his plane was shot down in a round of friendly fire. Although badly burned, he was able to pull himself and three other men onto a raft, and all were saved. After the war, Taylor dedicated himself to enjoying the great outdoors. He broke his back on a ski jump, and broke it again when he jumped over a tennis net. Once, while hunting, the goose he shot fell from the sky and hit him in the chest, shaking loose cartilage in his sternum that left him with breathing problems for a year. On a fly-fishing expedition, he slipped and fell into the Missouri River, but was pulled to safety by rescuers. In his later years, Taylor ran a small business selling firewood to his friends, until one day in 2005, a tree fell on top of him. After eighty-five long and wonderful years, John Taylor had finally had his last accident.

David Frazer survived being thrown from his car when it rolled over several times on a New Zealand highway. As he lay sprawled in the middle of the road, grateful to be alive, he was run over by an oncoming trailer truck. The truck had swerved to avoid Frazer's overturned car.

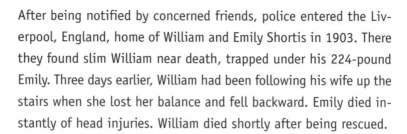

After being notified by concerned friends, police entered the Liverpool, England, home of William and Emily Shortis in 1903. There they found slim William near death, trapped under his 224-pound Emily. Three days earlier, William had been following his wife up the stairs when she lost her balance and fell backward. Emily died instantly of head injuries. William died shortly after being rescued.

In 1989, a false alarm indicating engine failure prompted the crew to bail out of a Soviet MiG-23 fighter jet that had just escaped from Poland. They put the plane on autopilot, put on their parachutes, and jumped out. They forgot to take with them the Belgian teenager they had just rescued.

The brilliant author, social critic, and religious leader, Thomas Merton, was lecturing in Bangkok in 1968. The oppressive heat and the man's advanced age quickly tired him, so he retired to his room immediately after the talk. He took a shower and then, still damp, went to turn on a small electric fan near his bed. About an hour later, a nun found him lying on the floor, naked, and on his back with the fan buzzing on his chest. He was still sizzling from the electric shock that had killed him.

In 1997, Karen Wetterhahn, a young scientist who had quietly achieved great success and respect in her field, was studying a man-made chemical called dimethylmercury. She took all the necessary precautions: gloves, goggles, a pristine work environment. A drop of the chemical fell on her gloved hand, and she promptly washed it off and proceeded with her work. What Ms. Wetterhahn had not yet had a chance to discover was that the chemical could pass through latex without making a visible hole. She died of mercury poisoning a year later.

Jane McDonald, a recently divorced seminary student, was staying at the home of a minister in Lanarkshire, Scotland, in 2003. While doing the dishes one evening, she slipped on the kitchen floor, fell headfirst into the dishwasher, and impaled herself on a kitchen knife.

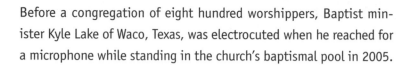

Before a congregation of eight hundred worshippers, Baptist minister Kyle Lake of Waco, Texas, was electrocuted when he reached for a microphone while standing in the church's baptismal pool in 2005.

When fire consumed a Dutch hospital in 2006, the surgical team had no time to take anything with them when they fled, not even the 69-year-old woman they had just strapped to the operating table. The woman had been given a mild sedative, but was still wide awake when the last of the operating room staff ran screaming from the room.

Ellen Shannon of Girard, Pennsylvania, died in 1870. She was killed in an explosion when she lit her oil lamp, which was full of R. E. Danforth's Non-Explosive Burning Fluid.

In 1927, famed dancer and lover of long scarves, Isadora Duncan, got into a convertible automobile and said, "Farewell, my friends! I go to glory!" The scarf she was wearing became entangled in the wheel of the car as it drove off, strangling her and breaking her neck.

Word got out that England was rehearsing for the funeral of the Queen Mother in 1993, prompting the Australian press to report a little too soon that she had already died. The Queen Mother, in fact, lived to see the new millennium, dying peacefully in her bed at the age of 101. Funeral rehearsals were conducted every six months or so in order to make the final spectacular tribute appear perfectly spontaneous. For the long-lived Queen Mother, the rehearsals went on for decades.

Newspapers all over the world printed the obituary of Dorothy Southworth Ritter in August 2001. The star of 1940s western movies, known also as Dorothy Fay, was the widow of singing cowboy Tex Ritter, and the mother of actor John Ritter. Ms. Ritter had been living in a nursing home after suffering a stroke. When a friend stopped by to visit, he was told Ms. Ritter was gone. The friend alerted the media, which put the obituary machine in motion. Ms. Ritter had, in fact, "gone" to another room in the facility.

In November 2003, all the newspapers reprinted her obituary after confirming that, this time, she really was gone.

During the filming of the 1995 movie, *Vampire in Brooklyn,* one scene called for Angela Bassett's character to jump from a building. Her stunt double, Sonja Davis, stepped in at the appropriate moment and took a beautiful backward dive into the alley, 45 feet below. She came *this close* to landing on the air bag.

In 2003, ten people died and more than seventy were injured in Santa Monica, California, when 89-year-old George Russell Weller's car plowed through a busy farmers' market. His attorneys called it "pedal error." Prosecutors claimed that Weller looked at what he had done, shrugged his shoulders, and said, "Oops."

CHAPTER

2

INESCAPABLE DESTINY

I'D RATHER GET MY BRAINS BLOWN OUT IN THE WILD

THAN WAIT IN TERROR AT THE SLAUGHTERHOUSE.

—Craig Volk

A VERY DEAR friend once told me, "All thought is creative; you cre-
ate what you think." So I've been trying very hard not to think
about newspaper headlines reading, AUTHOR OF WEIRD DEATHS BOOK DIES
IN FREAK ACCIDENT.

I don't know if there really is such a thing as predestination, or
if it's simply that our greatest fears are the very things most likely

to become self-fulfilling prophecies. Sigmund Freud argued that there was no such thing as a coincidence, that every act is deliberate whether we are conscious of it or not. Many devoutly religious people believe that every life is planned out to the last detail even before it is lived. Modern-day self-help gurus insist that we each possess the power to choose or change the course of our own lives.

Maybe they're all saying the same thing. Maybe they're all wrong. But maybe, just maybe, some of us end up getting killed by the very thing we've been avoiding all our lives.

I find that kind of funny.

Thinning the Herd

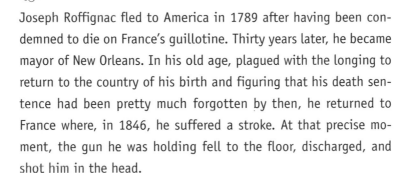

Joseph Roffignac fled to America in 1789 after having been condemned to die on France's guillotine. Thirty years later, he became mayor of New Orleans. In his old age, plagued with the longing to return to the country of his birth and figuring that his death sentence had been pretty much forgotten by then, he returned to France where, in 1846, he suffered a stroke. At that precise moment, the gun he was holding fell to the floor, discharged, and shot him in the head.

Hollywood movie star Natalie Wood suffered a lifelong fear of drowning. During the making of the 1961 movie *Splendor in the Grass,* director Elia Kazan had to cajole, comfort, and even lie to reassure Wood that she was in no danger during the filming of various scenes involving water. In 1981, from a yacht anchored off the coast of California, the actress fell into the water and drowned. The yacht's name was *The Splendor.*

Young movie starlet Linda Darnell developed a severe case of pyrophobia after having been burned on several occasions during movie shoots in the 1940s. She had also at one time suffered serious burns in a car accident. At the age of 41, while she was watching one of her old movies on late-night television, her house caught fire. Darnell was burned over 90 percent of her body. She died the next day.

The Flying ELVI is a daredevil skydiving team of Elvis Presley impersonators who rent themselves out for grand openings and all manner of over-the-top celebrations. Their act involves a dazzling combination of smoke trails, pyrotechnic fireworks, precision maneuvers, and the occasional splattered Elvis.

In 1996, one of the ELVI was blown off course as the troupe descended onto Boston Harbor. That Elvis died of his injuries. During a show in Montana in 2006, another Elvis broke most of his bones, including his pelvis, when he misjudged the landing and hit a concrete parking lot at 50 miles per hour. Yet another Elvis, who had given up the group because he found the experience thrilling but too dangerous, died in a plane crash in Ohio in 2003.

A pilot who survived a helicopter crash in the mountains of southwest Colombia in 1996 was thrilled to see the rescuers who arrived to save him from certain death. He was killed when he fell out of the rescue chopper.

A 60-year-old man identified only as Czeslaw B. from the Polish village of Kosianka-Trojanówka had an overwhelming fear of burglars. He booby-trapped every entrance and exit in his house, including the garage, which he outfitted with two homemade guns. He was killed in 1996 while opening the garage doors.

Texas pioneer Josiah P. Wilbarger was scalped by Comanches in 1833, but survived the attack. Despite his exposed skull, he lived well for eleven more years, until he bumped his head against a low beam in his cotton gin.

Composer Anton von Webern left Vienna during World War II, believing he would be safer in Mittersill, Austria. While standing on the veranda of his son-in-law's house, he was accidentally shot by a drunk American soldier.

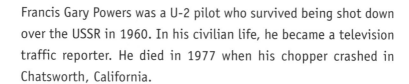

Francis Gary Powers was a U-2 pilot who survived being shot down over the USSR in 1960. In his civilian life, he became a television traffic reporter. He died in 1977 when his chopper crashed in Chatsworth, California.

Actor Jeffrey Hunter had a lot of trouble getting cast in other roles after playing Jesus Christ in the 1961 movie *King of Kings*. He acted mostly in small European productions and on television. In the meantime, he suffered a series of head injuries. He was hit by an exploding prop, was accidentally karate-chopped in the head, and had at least one seizure. A few days after being diagnosed with a displaced vertebra at the age of 42, he collapsed while climbing a flight of stairs in his house and hit his head again, this time fatally.

Bob Cartwright could not believe how close he came to dying in October 2006. His friend Tyler Stanger had offered him a seat on his small plane to see a Yankees game in New York. Stanger and Yankees pitcher Corey Lidle were killed instantly when they accidentally flew the plane into a Manhattan apartment building. One month later, Cartwright accepted a ride from two other friends. That small plane crashed into the shoreline of Big Bear Lake in California, killing all three men on board.

During the filming of the Chuck Norris action movie *Braddock: Missing in Action III* in the Philippines, a helicopter crash killed three extras. Two years later, Chuck returned to the Philippines to shoot another movie, *Delta Force 2*. This time, the helicopter crash killed five people. Apparently having learned nothing from their first tragic experience, the crew used a helicopter that had been repossessed by a bank and had been sitting in the hot tropical climate for several years.

The 1955 film *Rebel Without a Cause* was the story of troubled teens caught in a violent world of their own creation and their inability to connect with the older generation. Four of the movie's stars died tragically at a young age: James Dean died in a car crash. Natalie Wood drowned. Sal Mineo was murdered. Nick Adams overdosed on drugs.

King Henry II of France arranged for a three-day jousting tournament in 1559 to take place during his daughter's wedding celebration. In a famous quatrain issued one year before, Nostradamus had warned the king not to engage in jousts or combats of any kind:

> *The Lion shall overcome the old*
> *on the field of war in a single combat (duelle);*
> *He will pierce his eyes in a cage of gold*
> *This is the first of two lappings, then he dies a cruel death.*

Ignoring the warning, the King went forward with his plans and engaged in a joust with Gabriel Montgomery, a captain with the Scottish Guard. Montgomery's lance tip broke off in the soft golden grille of King Henry's helmet, piercing his eye and lodging in his brain. The King died eleven days later.

The first Canadian to conquer Niagara Falls in a barrel was a man named Karel Soucek. He took the plunge in July of 1984 and survived. He then went on tour demonstrating his technique. While re-creating the drop from a platform inside the Houston Astrodome, the barrel hit the edge of the water tank. Soucek was killed on impact.

During the final test flight of a new Douglas DC-7B airliner in 1957, the plane ran almost head-on into a U.S. Air Force F-89J Scorpion jet fighter. The pilots were able to swerve and missed each other, but they lost control of their respective planes and crashed. One of those killed was a copilot named Archie R. Twitchell. He was an actor who appeared in more than seventy films, including *I Wanted Wings* and *Among the Living*.

Flaming pieces of the wreckage fell onto a junior high school playground. One of the three students killed on the ground was a good friend of Richard Valenzuela, who would skyrocket to fame as rock-and-roll singer Ritchie Valens less than two years later. Having witnessed the carnage firsthand, Valens developed a horrendous fear of airplanes. The one and only time he ever got into a plane, it too crashed, killing him, Buddy Holly, J. P. Richardson (also known as The Big Bopper), and everyone else on board.

In his youth, novelist, philosopher, and Nobel Prize laureate Albert Camus once remarked that the most absurd way to die would be in a car accident. Many years later, in 1960, the nephew of his publisher managed to talk him into riding with him on a trip to Paris. The car swerved off the road and crashed into a tree, killing them both. The medical examiner at the morgue later found a train ticket to Paris in Camus's pocket.

Author George Bernard Shaw once said, "Life does not cease to be funny when people die." He died in 1950 at the age of 94, when he fell out of an apple tree.

The soul singer and songwriter Donnie Hathaway loved leaning out the window of his seventeen-story apartment in Chicago, preaching and singing to the crowds below. He also liked preaching from hotel windows whenever he was on tour, and was frequently asked to leave the premises. In January 1979, Hathaway leaned out a little too far and fell to his death from the fifteenth floor of New York's Essex Hotel. It is unclear whether he fell, jumped, or was pushed.

Hugh Gravitt was the off-duty cab driver who splattered Margaret Mitchell all over the streets of Atlanta in 1949. Fans of the famous author of *Gone with the Wind* never forgave him. When Gravitt was arrested immediately following the accident, police chief Herbert Jenkins demanded that he be charged with murder. Gravitt lived the rest of his life as a pariah.

Before the unfortunate event, Gravitt already had a long list of traffic violations under his belt. He was only 28 years old and had been driving for ten years, but had been ticketed on at least twenty-nine different occasions.

The jury found Gravitt guilty of involuntary manslaughter. The judge allowed him one week of freedom before handing down the sentence. The very next evening, he crashed his car into a truck, injuring himself and his wife. He was driving the same car that had killed Margaret Mitchell.

Comic book illustrator Dave Cockrum died in bed in 2006 wearing Superman pajamas and covered in a Batman blanket. He was cremated dressed in a Green Lantern shirt.

CNN announced to the world that rock musician Kurt Cobain had died of a drug overdose in Rome in March 1994. The news agency had to retract the story, of course, but not for long. Cobain blew his own brains out in Seattle just one month later. In his suicide note, he quoted Neil Young: "Better to burn out than to fade away."

Thuy Trang became famous in the 1990s playing "Trini Kwan" in *The Mighty Morphin' Power Rangers*. After a car accident in 1997, he was mistakenly reported dead. Trang survived that accident, but died in another car crash four years later.

Stella Chambers, an 85-year-old New Orleans resident, was looking forward to moving back into her restored redbrick house a year and a half after Hurricane Katrina had ripped it to shreds in 2005. Stella had been living in a flimsy FEMA trailer, and was waiting for just one more utility hookup before finally being able to move back into her own home. On the morning of February 13, 2007, a series of tornadoes ripped through what was left of New Orleans, flattening Stella's newly renovated house and the trailer in which she was living. Tragically, Stella's body was found inside the trailer later that day.

Thinning the Herd

John Wilkes Booth, Abraham Lincoln's assassin, enlisted in the Confederate Army only so that he could witness the hanging of abolitionist John Brown. As soon as that was done, he went back to his career as a mediocre actor. However, he continued his affiliation with sympathizers of the Confederacy, and believed he would ultimately prevail as a hero of the cause.

After shooting the president, Booth jumped off the theater balcony and broke his leg when he landed on the floor below. He managed to limp outside and mount his horse, and headed toward Maryland. He stopped at several places along the way, seeking sanctuary and medical assistance, but was repeatedly turned away by his fellow Confederates. Interestingly, it was a black farmer who helped him cross the Zekiah Swamp to the home of Samuel Cox, who also turned him away.

Booth finally found refuge in a barn owned by southerner Richard Garrett. Authorities closed in and set fire to some hay to smoke the assassin out. When he emerged from the barn, an officer raised his gun, aiming for Booth's arm. Booth made a jerking movement just as the officer pulled the trigger. The bullet hit Booth in the head, in very nearly the same spot as where Booth had shot the president.

As he lay dying, Booth uttered these words: "Tell Mother I died for my country. Useless! Useless!"

In 1988, businessman Paul Alarab tied a large trash can to a 60-foot rope, dangled it over the side of San Francisco's Golden Gate Bridge, and got in. His intention was to call attention to the plight of the elderly and the handicapped. His weight caused the rope to snap, and Alarab went plummeting to the icy waters below. Miraculously, he lived, becoming only one of twenty-six people ever to survive a plunge from the Golden Gate Bridge. He later told people that, on the way down, he begged God to give him one more chance. Alarab vowed never to put his life on the line like that again.

But there he was, fifteen years later, doing it again. Alarab once again strolled along the bridge's walkway and put his plan in motion. This time, he was protesting the U.S. invasion of Iraq. He carefully lowered himself to the other side of the railing, and tied himself with a rope to the outside of the bridge. He told would-be rescuers that he would climb back to safety once he could read a statement to the press. Camera crews quickly assembled at the scene, and Alarab read from his notes. About an hour later, disappointed that CNN had not sent a reporter, he placed his notes on the ledge, put his cell phone on top of the papers, unwound his wrist from the rope, and jumped.

It is impossible to know if Alarab meant to jump from the outset, if he changed his mind after standing so long on the "Bridge of Sighs" and succumbed to its legendary siren's call, or if he prayed again on his way down. What is certain is that his first plea was granted as requested: He asked for, and received, just one more chance.

Upon hearing of his father's suicide in 1928, Ernest Hemingway skulked away in disgust, calling the man a coward. The elder Hemingway had shot himself with an heirloom Civil War revolver, given to him by his own father. Three decades later, Hemingway himself would put a 12-gauge shotgun in his mouth and pull the trigger.

In the decades that followed, more Hemingways would perish in strange and certain ways. Ernest's sister, Ursula, died of a drug overdose in 1966 after finding out she had cancer. His brother, Leicester, shot himself in 1982. Hemingway's famous supermodel granddaughter, Margaux, died in 1995 after ingesting a lethal dose of prescription medication. Hemingway's youngest son, Gregory, a former doctor, author, and transsexual, was found dead in 2001, in his cell in a woman's prison, after having been arrested for indecent exposure in Florida.

A scene in the 1974 film *Dirty Mary Crazy Larry* had to be rewritten when actor Vic Morrow refused to get into a helicopter. "I have a premonition that I'm going to get killed in a helicopter crash," he said. Ten years later, Morrow was hacked to pieces by a helicopter rotor during the making of *Twilight Zone: The Movie*.

Mark Twain was born in 1835 as Halley's Comet passed close to the Earth. He felt certain all his life that, because he had come in with Halley, he would also go out with it. Sure enough, he died in 1910, when the comet was once again visible from Earth.

Three weeks before she died, Florida newscaster Christine Chubbuck asked the station's news director if she could write a piece on suicide. On the morning of July 15, 1974, she went on the air, read the first few news articles, and made the following announcement: "And now, in keeping with Channel 40's policy of always bringing you the latest in blood and guts, in living color, you're about to see another first: an attempted suicide." She then pulled out a .38-caliber revolver loaded with hollow-point bullets, and shot herself in the head on live TV.

The story she had written in longhand three weeks earlier was a faithful account of the events as they actually played out in real life. Of course, the self-inflicted gunshot on live television was more plan than premonition, but the description of the aftermath was eerily accurate, including being taken specifically to Sarasota Memorial Hospital, where she would be listed in critical condition and later pronounced dead.

Magician and comedian Tommy Cooper wowed British audiences for many years with his deliberately bumbling illusions and quasi-death-defying feats. During a live television broadcast in 1984 at Her Majesty's Theatre in Britain, Cooper dropped dead of a heart attack in the middle of his show. The crowd cheered. They thought it was part of the act.

Austrian composer Arnold Schoenberg suffered horrendous panic attacks because of his triskaidekaphobia (fear of the number thirteen). He was born on September 13, 1874. He died of fright on Friday the 13th, in July of 1951. At the time of his death, he was 76 years old (7 + 6 = 13).

CHAPTER

3

HOW THE MIGHTY
HAVE FALLEN

I AM READY TO MEET MY MAKER. WHETHER MY MAKER IS PREPARED

FOR THE GREAT ORDEAL OF MEETING ME IS ANOTHER MATTER.

Winston Churchill (1874–1965)

IT'S NOT THAT I like to snicker into my sleeve when I hear that some famously bombastic fool has met an appropriately embarrassing end. Well, yes, I do, a little, but I also find it rather fascinating how well Death puts Life into perspective.

Death is, after all, the great equalizer. It doesn't care what our day-to-day circumstances were, whether we were meek or mighty, rich or poor, tender or cruel. We are all, in that final moment, equally capable of meeting death with great dignity, with one last fabulous flourish of panache, or with a great big messy pant-load of fear for somebody else to clean up later.

In 1779, the natives of the Sandwich Islands so loved and admired their "discoverer" Captain James Cook that they stabbed him several dozen times, put him on a big stick, roasted him, and served him for dinner. The portions they did not eat that night were salted and preserved as leftovers. Afterward, they took back their islands' original name: Hawaii.

João Rodrigues Cabrilho was the swashbuckling sixteenth-century explorer who discovered California. In a dashing display of bravado, he leapt from one of his ships, sword in hand, to join in the fight against the hostile natives. He broke his leg in the fall and died of gangrene.

Attila the Hun was one of history's most notorious villains. By the year AD 450, he had conquered all of Asia, destroying every village in his path and pillaging the countryside from Mongolia to the outer edges of the Russian Empire. He died of a nosebleed on his wedding night.

Pope Formosus, head of the Catholic Church between 891 and 896, was one of relatively few people tried and convicted in a court of law after they were already dead. Formosus's political enemies exhumed his corpse, propped him up on a throne, dressed him in full papal regalia, and tried him on charges of perjury and other offenses. A church deacon answered for the corpse. Formosus's holiness was declared invalid and all of his acts as Pope were nullified. They even cut off his consecration fingers so he couldn't bless anyone in the afterlife. Formosus's corpse was then thrown into a grave, but later pulled out and thrown into the Tiber River.

It took W. C. Fields a rather long time to die. Years of boozing had decimated his liver, as well as many of his other internal organs. Fields's last coherent words tidily summed up the famous curmudgeon's attitudes about everything: "God damn the whole friggin' world and everyone in it but you, Carlotta!" This made the love of his life, Carlotta, very happy indeed. His wife, Hattie, on the other hand, was none too pleased.

Three things distinguished the short reign of Alexander I of Greece: He ascended the throne when his father abdicated in 1917, he became king before his older brother (it usually works the other way around), and his role was mostly ceremonial (the prime minister wielded the real power). However, Alexander will most likely be remembered for the manner in which he died: He was attacked by his gardener's monkey. The bite wounds became infected, and Alexander died of sepsis.

Al Capone, arguably the most notorious American gangster of all time, was a longtime member of the FBI's Ten Most Wanted list. His involvement in the murders of countless rivals and perceived enemies, illegal gambling, prostitution, and bootlegging was the stuff of legend. Despite numerous attempts to bring him to justice for his crimes, he was ultimately prosecuted and found guilty of tax evasion. While serving time in a maximum security prison, he died of syphilis.

Anton Joseph Cermak, mayor of Chicago, was accidentally assassinated while riding with president-elect Franklin Roosevelt in a motorcade. The president was unharmed.

The obscure and perplexing German philosopher Georg Hegel remained so to the very end. While on his deathbed in 1831, he said, "Only one man ever understood me, and even he didn't understand me."

At the wake of legendary Hollywood film producer Samuel Goldwyn, his partner Louis B. Mayer remarked, "The reason so many people showed up at the funeral was because they wanted to make sure he was dead." On his own deathbed in 1957, Mayer's last words were, "Nothing matters. Nothing matters."

General John Sedgwick, Union commander, was killed in battle during the U.S. Civil War. His last words were, "They couldn't hit an elephant at this dist—"

Thinning the Herd

After having been shot in battle, Mexican revolutionary Pancho Villa turned to a journalist who was nearby and shouted, "Don't let it end like this! Tell them I said something!"

William Harris Wharton, member of the Texas Republic Senate from 1836 to 1839, died when he accidentally shot himself while dismounting from his horse.

Richardson A. Scurry, a general in the Confederate Army during the Civil War, shot himself in the foot while hunting. The wound never healed. Although his leg was later amputated, he died as a result.

New York County representative Michael Edelstein delivered an impassioned speech on the floor of the U.S. House of Representatives in 1941, and dropped dead in the cloakroom immediately afterward.

Clement Laird Vallandigham was an attorney and a member of the Ohio State House of Representatives. He had been hired as a defense lawyer by an accused murderer in 1846. While preparing for a dramatic courtroom demonstration, Vallandigham accidentally shot himself dead.

James Collinsworth was one of the signers of the Texas Declaration of Independence and a candidate for the presidency of the Republic of Texas in 1838. After a week of drunken excess during his presidential campaign, he jumped off a boat into Galveston Bay and drowned.

R. Budd Dwyer, member of the Pennsylvania State House of Representatives from 1965 to 1970, was convicted in December 1986 of bribery and conspiracy in federal court. About to be sentenced and widely expected to resign from office, he called a press conference. There, in front of spectators and television cameras, he insisted that he was not guilty, and pulled out a gun. "This thing will hurt someone," he said, then shot himself dead.

Thinning the Herd

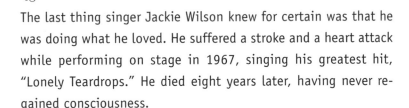

The last thing singer Jackie Wilson knew for certain was that he was doing what he loved. He suffered a stroke and a heart attack while performing on stage in 1967, singing his greatest hit, "Lonely Teardrops." He died eight years later, having never regained consciousness.

Ancient Greek dramatist, Aeschylus, who once wrote, "O Death the Healer, scorn thou not . . . Pain lays not its touch upon a corpse," was killed when a giant vulture-like bird dropped a turtle on his head.

Poet and grammarian Philetas of Cos is said to have died of insomnia in 270 BC. He drove himself crazy trying to figure out the Liar Paradox ("I am lying now. This statement is false.")

In 121 BC, the Roman Senate wanted a powerful public speaker named Gaius Gracchus dead. The Senate set as a bounty the weight of Gracchus's head in gold. One of the coconspirators, Septimuleius, decapitated Gracchus, scooped out his brains, and filled the skull with molten lead. Septimuleius was paid in full: seventeen pounds of gold.

🐍

Ben Klassen was at one time a Florida state legislator. He was also the man who invented the electric can opener. However, he achieved his greatest success in 1973, when he founded the Church of the Creator and became a huge magnet for neo-Nazis and white supremacists from all over the world. When one of his followers killed a Persian Gulf War veteran in 1993, the family of the murdered soldier filed suit against the church. Klassen sold the compound, then blew his own brains out.

🐍

In the year AD 260, the Roman emperor Valerian was defeated in battle and captured by the Persians. King Shapur I turned him into a human footstool. After many years of this humiliation, Valerian offered the king a large ransom for his release. In response, Shapur had molten gold poured down Valerian's throat. Shapur then had Valerian skinned, and the skin stuffed with straw and preserved as a trophy in the main Persian temple. Only after Persia's defeat in their last war with Rome 350 years later was Valerian's skin cremated and given proper burial.

One of the things that best exemplifies the difference between humans and the rest of the animal kingdom is our love of ceremony. Certain ancient nomadic tribes, for example, would sacrifice a white horse when the leader of their tribe died. When the Hungarian chieftain Álmos led his tribe to utter defeat in the Pecheneg invasion of AD 895, he was killed by his own people. The execution was immediately followed by the traditional horse sacrifice.

Holy Roman Emperor Frederick I, en route to the Third Crusade, stopped at the banks of the Saleph River for a cool drink of water. Stooped over, he suffered a heart attack. The weight of his armor pulled him facedown into the riverbank. He drowned in water that was just a few inches deep.

King Louis II of Hungary also drowned in a shallow stream under the weight of his own armor. Louis, however, was not heading bravely into battle at the time. He was fleeing the Ottomans after leading his army to utter defeat in the Battle of Mohács in 1526.

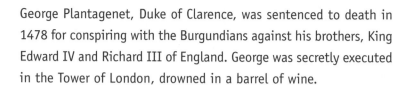

George Plantagenet, Duke of Clarence, was sentenced to death in 1478 for conspiring with the Burgundians against his brothers, King Edward IV and Richard III of England. George was secretly executed in the Tower of London, drowned in a barrel of wine.

Pope Clement VII died in 1534 after eating the death cap mushroom. It is widely believed he was deliberately poisoned.

Pedro de Valdivia, the dreaded sixteenth-century Spanish conquistador, was captured and killed by Native Americans. They poured molten gold down his throat to satisfy his thirst for their treasures.

In 1799, Constantine Hangerli, Prince of Wallachia, was arrested by a Kapucu and a Moor, and sentenced to multiple executions. He was strangled, shot, stabbed, and decapitated, all in rapid succession.

Thinning the Herd

William Henry Harrison, ninth president of the United States, refused to wear a coat to his inaugural speech, despite the fact that it was unusually cold in Washington, D.C., that day in March 1841. Harrison's presidential address, the longest in American history, included the promise that he would not seek a second term in office. He kept his promise by dying of pneumonia one month later.

Zachary Taylor, twelfth president of the United States, while attending the laying of the cornerstone of the Washington Monument on an exceptionally hot and humid Fourth of July, quickly consumed large quantities of iced milk, cold cherries, and pickled cucumbers. He died of uncontrollable diarrhea five days later.

Beloved Empress Elisabeth (Sissi) of Austria was long considered one of the world's most beautiful women. She sustained the image through decades-long starvation diets and obsessive exercise, which resulted in severe malnutrition, depression, and suicidal fantasies.

While she was strolling on the promenade along Lake Geneva in 1898, a crazed Italian anarchist stabbed her with a needle-thin file. She had been so severely strapped into her corset that she hardly noticed. She walked a dozen or so steps and asked, "What happened to me?" And then she died.

It seemed that the enemies of the last Tsar of Russia would never succeed in assassinating Grigory Rasputin, the Russian mystic, friend, and advisor to the Romanovs. The conspirators poisoned him, bludgeoned him, and shot him in the head, lungs, and liver. Rasputin was still alive when he was dumped in the Neva River. He drowned when he became trapped under the ice.

Barcelona's superstar architect, Antoni Gaudí, was run over by a streetcar in 1926. He was very shabbily dressed at the time, and cab drivers refused requests from bystanders to take "the poor vagabond" to the hospital. Gaudí died in a pauper's clinic a few days later. When it was discovered that the "bum" was in fact the venerated Gaudí, police fined all the cab drivers.

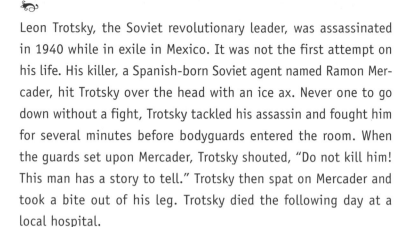

Leon Trotsky, the Soviet revolutionary leader, was assassinated in 1940 while in exile in Mexico. It was not the first attempt on his life. His killer, a Spanish-born Soviet agent named Ramon Mercader, hit Trotsky over the head with an ice ax. Never one to go down without a fight, Trotsky tackled his assassin and fought him for several minutes before bodyguards entered the room. When the guards set upon Mercader, Trotsky shouted, "Do not kill him! This man has a story to tell." Trotsky then spat on Mercader and took a bite out of his leg. Trotsky died the following day at a local hospital.

Vlad Înecatul, sixteenth-century Prince of Wallachia and descendant of Vlad the Impaler (fictionalized by Bram Stoker as Count Dracula), got drunk one night and rode his horse into the waters of the Dâmbovița River. He fell off the horse and drowned.

President James Garfield lay dying after having been shot by a would-be assassin. Alexander Graham Bell rushed to the president's side with one of his new inventions: the metal detector. It did not occur to the brilliant inventor until much later that the device could not tell the difference between a bullet and a bed-spring. Garfield died of septicemia (an infection in the blood) after having suffered multiple incisions at the hands of his doctor, who kept opening Garfield up in all the wrong places, guided by Bell and his machine in search of the bullet.

King Henry I of Castile ascended to the Spanish throne at a very young age. Dubbed Henry the Sufferer, his short and unremarkable reign ended suddenly when a roof tile fell on his head in 1217.

Emperor Louis the Pious, son of the great Charlemagne, King of the Francs, was literally scared to death when he experienced five minutes of total darkness during the lunar eclipse of May 5, 840.

After having ridden on horseback for several hours in the cold and snow, George Washington returned home exhausted and with a severe case of laryngitis. He was given a concoction of molasses, vinegar, and butter and told to gargle. A preparation of dried beetles was also placed on his throat, and four and a half liters of blood were extracted within a twenty-four-hour period (bloodletting was still a very common practice in the 1700s). George Washington had survived the American Revolution, the nation's first presidency, and innumerable armed and political battles, but died of his own doctor's ministrations.

Sir Arthur Aston was a royal army officer during the First English Civil War. He became governor of Oxford in 1643 and promptly made himself unpopular, not for the first time. He regained some of the people's goodwill when he lost a leg after falling from a horse in 1644. Five years later, during the Siege of Drogheda in Ireland led by Oliver Cromwell and his troops, Aston was beaten to death with his own wooden leg.

Two and a half years after the death of Oliver Cromwell in 1658, he was exhumed, tried, found guilty of treason, and executed all over again. Cromwell's corpse was hanged, and then decapitated for good measure. His body was thrown into a pit, and his head stuck on a pole. The moldering head-on-a-stick was on display in front of Westminster Abbey for more than twenty-five years.

For the next three centuries, Cromwell's head would exchange hands repeatedly as a gruesomely sought-after collector's item. It was finally bequeathed to Cambridge College in 1960, where it was buried near Sidney Sussex Chapel.

Constans II of the Byzantine Empire ordered the murder of his brother, Theodosius, to prevent him from succeeding to the throne. Detested by his own people for the fratricide, Constans was killed in his own bathtub by one of his attendants. The chamberlain broke a marble soap dish over the emperor's head.

Pope John XXI was an ophthalmologist before entering religious life. In his first year as Pope, he ordered a special laboratory built on the grounds of the Vatican so that he could work in relative peace and quiet. During construction in 1277, the building collapsed on top of him, ending his short reign.

Thinning the Herd

King Béla I of Hungary fought a successful war against Holy Roman Emperor Henry III to defend his country's independence. Béla died when the canopy of his tall wooden throne collapsed on top of him in 1063.

In the 1960s race between the United States and the Soviet Union to develop the first intercontinental ballistic missile, Soviet Red Army marshal Mitrofan Nedelin gruffly dismissed his technicians' warnings and ordered them to forge ahead with preparations to launch the first R-16 rocket. Nedelin set up a chair at the launchpad to better oversee the operations. As predicted, the missile exploded, instantly incinerating Nedelin and everyone else in the immediate area. They were the lucky ones. Dozens of others were also killed in the explosion, but most of them died slow, miserable deaths because they were a little farther away.

The official cause of death of King Edward II of England in 1327 was recorded as "a foreign object" (a red-hot poker) "entering the body" (shoved, actually) "through the skin or natural orifice" (his butt).

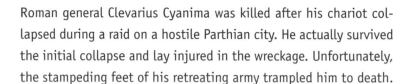

Roman general Clevarius Cyanima was killed after his chariot collapsed during a raid on a hostile Parthian city. He actually survived the initial collapse and lay injured in the wreckage. Unfortunately, the stampeding feet of his retreating army trampled him to death.

Sir Walter Raleigh led an incredible life of accomplishment. He was a poet, a historian, an explorer, a philosopher, and a soldier. It was that last thing that kept getting him into trouble, though. Raleigh was sentenced to death in 1603 for treason and imprisoned in the Tower of London. He was granted a reprieve in 1619, but that turned out to be short-lived. Two years later, Raleigh attacked a Spanish camp near the Orinoco River in South America, and was re-sentenced to death. It took the executioner two tries before he could separate Raleigh from his head.

Raleigh's wife had his head embalmed. She kept it in a red leather bag until her own death twenty-nine years later.

At a meeting with his advisors, Sobhuza II, King of Swaziland, abruptly stopped the discussion and dismissed everyone from the room, except for his minister of health. Sobhuza said to the man, "I am going." The minister asked, "Where?" Sobhuza smiled, waved good-bye, and dropped dead.

The ancient Greek philosopher Socrates was found guilty of corrupting the morals of minors and was sentenced to death by poison. Before taking the drink of hemlock, Socrates turned to his friend, Crito, and said, "I owe Asclepius a cock. Will you remember to pay the debt?"

Simón Bolívar, the great soldier and statesman who successfully led the revolution against Spanish rule in South America, died on a hammock while visiting a friend in 1830. Shortly before expiring, he commented, "The three biggest fools that have ever lived are Christ, Don Quixote, and me."

Distraught over the severe criticism he was receiving for his novel, *Finnegan's Wake,* author James Joyce asked before dying, "Really? Does no one understand?"

Galileo Galilei published a number of astronomical findings that happened to contradict the Church's teachings. He was condemned as a heretic and spent the rest of his life under house arrest. In mortal fear of the sadistic wrath with which the Church conducted itself during the Inquisition, he agreed to publicly recant all that he knew.

On his deathbed in 1642, and having nothing left to lose, Galileo proclaimed, "I don't care what they say! The Earth *does* revolve around the sun!"

A mere 350 years later, the Church quietly admitted that perhaps Galileo was correct. Some Catholic scholars, however, are still investigating.

Albert Einstein spoke his last words on his deathbed, but we will never know what they were. His nurse didn't speak German.

Billy the Kid suddenly sat up and asked, "Who's there?" To which sheriff Pat Garrett responded with a bullet to the bad boy's heart.

While sleeping in a dark room, the outlaw Billy the Kid suddenly sat up and asked, "Who's there?" To which sheriff Pat Garrett responded with a bullet to the bad boy's heart.

Thinning the Herd

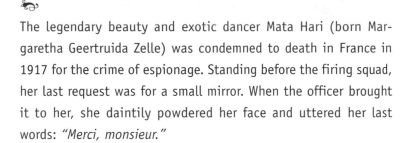

The legendary beauty and exotic dancer Mata Hari (born Margaretha Geertruida Zelle) was condemned to death in France in 1917 for the crime of espionage. Standing before the firing squad, her last request was for a small mirror. When the officer brought it to her, she daintily powdered her face and uttered her last words: *"Merci, monsieur."*

Burmese kings seem to have been particularly unfortunate in the manner of their deaths. Three of them were trampled by elephants. One was killed by an enraged farmer after the king ate his cucumbers.

Author Virginia Woolf filled her pockets full of rocks one day in 1941, and walked into the River Ouse in Sussex, England. Her body finally washed up on the shallow banks of the river eighteen days later.

In what was certainly one of the most gruesome and inhumane executions in the history of the world, György Dózsa was captured after leading the peasants' revolt against the Kingdom of Hungary in 1514. In mockery of his ambition to be king, his sadistic captors sat him on a white-hot iron throne and placed an equally hot iron crown on his head and scepter in his hand. Dózsa was effectively roasted alive. Half-cooked and still conscious, six of Dózsa's fellow rebels, who had been starved by their captors for a week, were made to devour their leader. Dózsa reportedly endured this horrifically torturous death with the same dignity and stoicism with which he lived.

President Harry Truman left instructions indicating that he wanted to be buried in a casket of mulberry wood because, he said, "I want to go through hell a-cracklin' and a-poppin'!"

In 1998, Nigerian dictator Sani Abacha arranged an orgy in his home with a couple of local prostitutes. He took some Viagra to get things started, and suffered a massive heart attack in the middle of the party.

Thinning the Herd

Harold Holt, the prime minister of Australia in 1967, went for a swim in the waters near Melbourne one warm December day in 1967. "I know this beach like the back of my hand," he told a companion before he went into the water. He was never seen or heard from again.

Republican R. Budd Dwyer was facing up to fifty-five years in prison for his involvement in a bribery scandal in 1987. The Pennsylvania state treasurer called a news conference in his office the day before sentencing. Before an entire contingent of reporters and with television cameras rolling, Dwyer put a revolver in his mouth and pulled the trigger.

Dwyer's family received $1.28 million in pension benefits because, technically, the felon had not yet been sent to jail.

Dr. Eugene Shoemaker was the astronomer who codiscovered the Comet Shoemaker-Levy 9. He died in a car accident in 1997. His ashes were put on the *Lunar Prospector* space probe, and buried on the moon. He is the only person thus far to be laid to rest there.

The Crown Prince Dipendra of Nepal was not particularly pleased with his parents' choice for a bride. He was madly in love with another woman. He entered the billiards room after dinner one night in 2001, drunk and heavily armed. He went on a rampage and massacred most of the royal family. Dipendra himself died four days later from wounds he received from the palace guards trying to subdue him. Officials of the royal court insisted that all of the killings were accidental.

Ruthless King James I of Scotland liked to spend much of his leisure time on the tennis courts of a Dominican monastery in Perth. Frustrated over losing so many balls through an opening near the courts, he ordered the area sealed. The following day, plotters broke into his room to assassinate him. He climbed through a sewer passageway to escape, and was murdered by Sir Robert Graham at the dead end formed by the seal he himself had ordered the previous day.

Orville Redenbacher, the popcorn king, might have survived his heart attack in 1995 if not for the fact that he was taking a bath at the time. He drowned in his own bathtub.

Thinning the Herd

Dr. Nnamdi Azikiwe, known affectionately as Zik of Africa, was the first president of Nigeria. In 1996, he was reported dead by a newspaper in his homeland several days before his actual death at age 91.

As the Pope lay dying of pneumonia in 1922, a New York City newspaper ran the headline POPE BENEDICT XV IS DEAD. When alerted of the error, the paper changed the headline in the next edition to read POPE HAS MIRACULOUS RECOVERY.

Obituary writers at London's *The Daily Telegraph* jumped the gun a bit when they reported that Cockie Hoogterp had been killed in a car accident. Cockie was the second wife of Baron Bror Blixen-Finecke. It was, in fact, the baron's third wife who had been killed the crash. His first wife, Karen von Blixen-Finecke (also known as the author Isak Dinesen), had died her own weird death decades earlier.

Cockie began returning all of her bills marked DECEASED and demanded that the *Telegraph* publish the following statement: "Mrs.

Hoogterp wishes it to be known that she has not yet been screwed in her coffin."

When Cockie really did die, her obituary in the *Telegraph* said of her, "Few women, other than the very rich, can have survived into the late 1980s without ever having boiled an egg or made her own bed."

The author Isak Dinesen, perhaps best known for her novel *Out of Africa* and whose real name was Karen von Blixen-Finecke, liked telling people that her husband, Baron Bror Blixen-Finecke, who was also her second cousin, had contracted syphilis through one of his many extramarital dalliances and had given it to her in their first year of marriage. Far from considering the disease a source of shame, and despite the fact that she was convinced she would die of it, she rather liked having syphilis. In her view of the world, it was the disease of poets and heroes. It was also the disease of her father, who, upon learning that he had become infected, chose to kill himself rather than risk giving it to his wife.

The baron apparently recovered from his symptoms without medication. Dinesen, on the other hand, consumed mercury and arsenic over a long period of time, which was the only known remedy in the early 1900s. Some medical scholars believe that it was the treatment, not the disease, which ultimately killed the brilliant author, who was twice nominated for a Nobel Prize.

In 1979, the nation of India went into a brief period of deep mourning, and then just as quickly came out of it. Parliament was suspended, schools were closed, and radio broadcasting went silent when it was announced that Prime Minister Jayaprakash Narayan had passed away. The PM was still alive, but just barely. He did die shortly thereafter. However, the nation waited twenty years—just to be sure—before honoring him with the India's Jewel Award.

John Stonehouse, a member of the British Parliament, might have gotten away with faking his own death, but he was a little too conspicuous for his own good. He left a pile of clothes on a beach in Miami, Florida, leading the FBI and other American authorities to conclude he had committed suicide. This theory made sense because it was well known that Stonehouse had some serious financial difficulties back home. Stonehouse entered Australia on the stolen passport of a dead constituent and lived lavishly in Melbourne, posing as an English aristocrat. The actual identity of the aristocrat was another dead Londoner. Australian authorities became suspicious when Stonehouse tried to open a bank account with the £600,000 he had embezzled from a charity fund intended for victims of a hurricane in Bangladesh.

Stonehouse's wife was ecstatic upon hearing the news that her husband was still alive. That quickly changed when she arrived in Australia to find him living with his beautiful former secretary.

Stonehouse served only three of the seven years to which he was sentenced. He was given an early release because of heart problems. He did live another twelve years after his release, giving him plenty of time to write his autobiography, *Death of an Idealist*. He died of a heart attack in 1988.

An English knight named Thomas FitzGerald was found guilty of treason in 1567. He was hanged, drawn, and quartered for his crime, as was the custom in those days. FitzGerald's mother then went about the sad business of gathering his body parts for burial, but first she drank the blood from his severed head.

In the first century BC, King Fjölnir of Ynglingatal awoke in the night with the urgent need to relieve himself. He had passed out in his chambers after a long night of drinking and merriment. Still suffering the effects of his inebriation, he got lost on the way back to his quarters. He stumbled, fell into a barrel of beer, and drowned.

The ancient Greek mathematician Archimedes was busy working out an equation, writing in the sand with a stick. The last words he ever spoke were "Don't disturb my circles." His fatal error was speaking those words to a Roman soldier.

French grammarian, Dominique Bouhours, was a stickler to the end. Her last words were, "I am about to—or I am going to—die. Either expression is correct."

In the last moments of her life in 1964, Lady Astor, the first female member of British Parliament, woke up from a light slumber only long enough to turn to the family members surrounding her deathbed and say, "Am I dying? Or is this my birthday?"

🐛

Gaius Julius Caesar Augustus was affectionately nicknamed Caligula ("Little Boots") by his father's soldiers, who loved seeing him as a little boy roaming the grounds in military attire. "Little Boots" grew up to become one of the cruelest and most debauched Roman emperors in a long line of cruel and debauched Roman emperors. He was stabbed to death by his own guards. Mortally wounded, he said to his killers, "I am still alive!" And then he died.

🐛

King George V, grandfather to Queen Elizabeth II, is best remembered for relinquishing all of his German titles during World War I and changing the family's name to Windsor. The stress of war took its toll on the king's health. He suffered pulmonary problems that were further exacerbated by his smoking habit. In January of 1936, he took to his bed complaining of a cold, but never recovered from the illness. His personal physician, Lord Dawson of Penn, decided there was no point in letting the king linger. Late in the evening of January 20, the doctor administered a lethal dosage of cocaine and morphine so that the king's death could be announced in the morning edition of *The Times of London*.

The king's last words were uttered to his nurse. He regained consciousness just long enough to yell at her, "God damn you!"

At the start of the French Revolution in the late eighteenth century, Thomas de Mahay, Marquis de Favras, was tricked into making arrangements to help King Louis XVI and Marie Antoinette escape the country, and then sentenced to hang for treason. A court clerk handed him the official death sentence. The marquis read it carefully and said to the clerk, "I see that you have made three spelling mistakes."

Henrik Ibsen was a brilliant and prolific playwright until he suffered a stroke in 1900 at the age of 72. After that, his marriage was described as "joyless" and his thinking "cloudy." As the end of his life neared, a friend who came to visit asked his housekeeper how Ibsen was holding up. The housekeeper said he was feeling a little better, to which Ibsen replied, "On the contrary!" and died.

The daring French philosopher Voltaire frequently refuted the fiercely held religious beliefs of his times, despite the strict censorship laws of eighteenth-century France. When a priest at his deathbed asked him to renounce Satan, he replied, "Now, now, dear man. This is not the time to be making enemies."

Helle Cristina Habsburg Windsor was considered by some to be an insufferable bore. She delighted especially in her claims of being a descendant of Spanish royalty. "I was born on the steps of the throne!" she intoned a few times too many. "So awkward for her mother," noted her obituary writer.

As Joan Crawford lay on her deathbed in 1977, her devoted housekeeper, assistant, and probably only true friend in the world, fell to her knees and began to pray out loud for the legendary actress. Crawford turned on her immediately. She propped herself up slightly and said, "Damn it, don't you dare ask God to help me!" She was dead before her head hit the pillow.

Thinning the Herd

In the last years of his life, the great American poet Walt Whitman searched the depths of his soul for something glorious, a few brilliant and patriotic words to leave behind as his legacy for all of humanity. He gave up, finally, uttering only one word before dying: "Shit."

CHAPTER

4

DEATH'S LITTLE
IRONIES

ACCORDING TO THOSE great academic thinkers who spend much of their lives figuring out such things, there are three kinds of irony: There is Tragic Irony, *as in the O. Henry story of the guy who sells his watch to buy his wife a pretty hair comb, only to discover that she has shaved her head nearly bald to sell her hair so she could buy him a chain for his watch.* Socratic Irony *occurs when a teacher, for example, pretends to be an idiot in order to force his students to come up with the correct answer on their own, or to prove to them that they really are stupid.* Cosmic Irony *comes from the belief that weird things happen to us for no other reason than the occasional amusement of the gods, and there is nothing we can do about it. These very same academics tend to look down their noses at one of the most interesting forms of irony.* Comic Irony, *they say dismissively, happens by accident, as when the unexpected outcome of a story "startles" us into laughter. That doesn't surprise me. Not a single one of my college professors was funny.*

Come to think of it, I learned the hard way that very few of their academic theories applied to the day-to-day realities and challenges of living and working in the world. I'm not bitter about that, though. I'm sure that, by now, most of them are dead.

Thinning the Herd

Jerome Irving Rodale was the founding father of the organic food movement. In 1971, he appeared on *The Dick Cavett Show* to discuss the importance of pesticide-free farming, and the health benefits of eating conscientiously grown foods. In the middle of the show, he died in his chair of a heart attack.

When Raymond Martinot and his longtime companion, Monique Leroy, envisioned the thawing of their cryogenically preserved bodies, they probably didn't imagine that the process would involve an oven.

Monique passed away in 1984, and Raymond immediately had her body frozen. He also made arrangements to have his own body preserved upon his death, which took place in 2002. The couple enjoyed years of postmortem celebrity as France's best-known aboveground corpses.

During a visit to his parents' not-quite-final resting place, the Martinots' son, Rémy, discovered that, at some point, the freezer had stopped working. He was forced to cremate the no-longer-frozen remains of his parents.

In 2004, Renaldo Appollis, a worker at a South African poultry plant, was hanging live chickens on the hooks of the conveyor system that transported them to the part of the machine that chopped their heads off. The hood of Appollis's overalls became entangled in the mechanism, thus causing him to suffer the same fate as his chickens: death by decapitation.

Dan Young lived just long enough to see the impossible happen: He was released from death row in 2005 after DNA evidence proved he was not a murderer. Shortly after his release, he was killed by a hit-and-run driver in Chicago.

Franz Riedl, of Austria, was very responsible with his money. He arranged for his rent and other bills to be paid automatically from his bank account every month. Riedl's mummified corpse lay undetected in his apartment for at least five years, until the funds ran out in his bank account in October 2006 and his landlord came to collect the overdue rent.

Thinning the Herd

Aleksis Kivi was the first professional writer to publish his works in Finnish. The effects of extreme poverty and schizophrenia resulted in an early death at age 38. Nine months after his last hospitalization in a mental ward, his brother had taken him to a small rented cottage, where Kivi spent his final weeks. On New Year's Eve, 1872, Kivi sat up and proclaimed, "I am alive!" and then he died.

William Brodie, a respected figure in Edinburgh, Scotland, was the creator of "The Drop"—the trapdoor on the floor of the gallows where condemned prisoners were hanged. Brodie was the first to try out his own invention. He was executed in 1788 for the crime of burglary.

Robert Case of Belle River, Ontario, had a long standing feud with Essex County authorities over an old tree stump he considered a safety hazard. For three years, he campaigned to have the stump removed from Lake St. Clair. He got little more than the runaround. In February 2007, he unequivocally proved his case once and for all when his snowmobile skidded and plowed right into the stump. Case was pronounced dead at the scene.

Death's Little Ironies

At the age of 17, First Lady Laura Bush was behind the wheel of a car when she ran a stop sign and hit another vehicle. The car she hit belonged to one of her classmates, who was killed in the accident. Although the incident rarely, if ever, comes to light, Mrs. Bush now dedicates her First-Ladyship to visiting schools, where she encourages children to "Stop and Think It Through," lecturing them on the importance of following safety rules.

Joaquin Laguer, a patron at a Brooklyn, New York, tattoo parlor, became dizzy, fainted, and fell headfirst into a display case. Laguer was nearly decapitated by the shattered glass, and bled to death before the ambulance could arrive. The tattoo he had selected was called "Last Rites."

A former schoolteacher and excommunicated Catholic priest named Joseph Kibweteere founded the Movement for the Restoration of the Ten Commandments of God. He told followers that the Virgin Mary came to him in a dream and told him the Apocalypse was scheduled for midnight on December 31, 1999, a fitting end to the "corruption of man."

As it turns out, no man was more corrupt than Kibweteere. When midnight came and went with nary a stir, Kibweteere rescheduled the Apocalypse for December 31, 2000. However, in March, he came up with a better plan. He gathered more than 600 church members and threw a huge party for them. He fed them lots of red meat and Coca-Cola, and then he set them all on fire.

Immediately after, Kibweteere fled the secluded compound with all the money and possessions his followers had been forced to siqn over to him when they joined his church. The 68-year-old cult leader was never found.

For one German tourist in 2006, "The Happiest Place on Earth" turned out to be the deadliest. A blood vessel burst in the 49-year-old woman's head while she was riding Mission: SPACE at Epcot, Walt Disney World, Florida. She died the following day in (of all places) Celebration Hospital.

A Scottish clan chieftain named Maelbrigte of Moray was nicknamed "The Tusk" for his large protruding teeth. In a battle with the Norwegians in the year AD 892, King Sigurd I of Orkney killed

Maelbrigte, then chopped off his head and strapped it to his saddle. As he rode, Maelbrigte's "tusk" scraped against Sigurd's leg. The wound soon became infected. Sigurd died of septic shock.

King Louis XIV of France put his best chef, François Vatel, in charge of the food preparations for an enormous three-day feast. Vatel ordered great quantities of seafood from fishmongers far and wide. When the first day of festivities arrived and no fish had yet been delivered, Vatel despaired. Certain he would never live down this disgrace, the chef went to his room, propped a sword against the door, and impaled himself through the heart. His body was discovered shortly afterward by a kitchen assistant who had come to notify Vatel that cartloads of fish were arriving from all corners of France.

In October 2005, a Hmong immigrant named Chai Soua Vang went hunting in northwestern Wisconsin, but bagged six deer hunters instead. Chai Soua Vang later told police that the other hunters were drunk, had accosted him with racial slurs, and had tried to shoot him first. He killed the hunters in self-defense, shooting some of them in the back.

Thinning the Herd

About a year later, another Hmong immigrant tangled with a squirrel hunter just north of Green Bay, Wisconsin. It didn't take very long for an argument between the two to escalate into violence. James Nichols (the squirrel hunter) told Cha Vang (no relation to Chai Soua Vang) that he was encroaching on his territory. Cha Vang disagreed. The two tried to settle the matter by screaming obscenities at each other. It ended with Nichols shooting Vang and stabbing him six times with his hunting knife.

It is very likely that Cha Vang died not knowing what the fight was about. Unlike Chai Soua Vang, Cha Vang spoke no English, and Nichols had no idea what Vang had been screaming at him.

In 1844, the battleship USS *Princeton* fired its cannons in salute to Secretary of State Abel P. Upshur, Secretary of the Navy Thomas Walker Gilmur, and other dignitaries among the two hundred people on board the ship that day. One of the cannons, whose design was later found to be seriously flawed, exploded. The blast killed Upshur, Gilmer, and several others. The cannon that fired the fatal salute was called The Peacemaker.

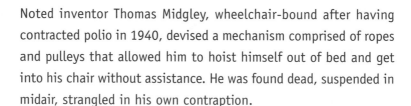

Noted inventor Thomas Midgley, wheelchair-bound after having contracted polio in 1940, devised a mechanism comprised of ropes and pulleys that allowed him to hoist himself out of bed and get into his chair without assistance. He was found dead, suspended in midair, strangled in his own contraption.

The Russian physician, philosopher, economist, science fiction writer, and revolutionary, Alexander Bogdanov, believed that human rejuvenation was possible through blood transfusions from young donors. Very little was known about transfusions in the early 1900s, but this didn't stop Bogdanov from experimenting on himself. After eleven transfusions, he happily reported that his eyesight had improved and he was no longer going bald. Unfortunately, the youthful blood of his last donor also contained malaria and tuberculosis, which killed him.

Famed baritone Leonard Warren suffered a stroke and collapsed on stage at the New York Metropolitan Opera in 1960. The opera was *La forza del destino* (The Force of Destiny). The last line he sang was, *"Morir? Tremenda cosa."* ("To die? A wondrous thing.")

Elisha Mitchell, geologist and explorer, slipped and died of a fall in 1857. He fell into Mitchell Falls in North Carolina, which he himself had named twenty-two years earlier. He is buried at the summit of Mount Mitchell.

Stephen Davidson, a 35-year-old member of a cult known as the Barry Long Foundation, was found dead in 2005 in Butleigh Woods in Glastonbury, England. The coroner found particles of yew leaf in Davidson's throat, which is known to cause problems in the heart and lungs. Next to his body were a pile of sacred pebbles and healing crystals.

Although Bobby Leach broke nearly every bone in his body, he survived a barrel ride over Niagara Falls in 1911. He made a full recovery and went on to travel the world, thrilling audiences with the tale of his adventure. While on tour, he suffered fatal injuries when he slipped on a fruit peel on a New Zealand sidewalk.

Medal of Honor winner Lloyd Hughes, a B-24 bomber pilot during World War II, managed to destroy enemy oil refineries in Romania even though his plane was severely damaged in the battle. He returned to the base a hero, but his plane exploded on landing.

James Douglas, the Earl of Morton, was executed in Scotland in 1581 for his role in the murder of the treacherous Henry Stuart, husband of Mary, Queen of Scots. Douglas was executed on The Maiden, a new and improved guillotine-like device that he himself had invented.

Tom Evans and Pete Ham, who were members of the popular band Badfinger, both committed suicide by hanging (Ham in 1975, and Evans in 1983). They were the authors of the song "Without You," which became a huge hit for Harry Nilsson, Mariah Carey, and Clay Aiken. The chorus of the song begins, "I can't live, I can't live anymore."

Reverend Jack Arnold was nothing if not a man of his word. While delivering a sermon one Sunday in 2005 in his Presbyterian church in Orlando, Florida, he looked out on his congregation and said, "When I go to heaven . . ." and promptly dropped dead.

Singer-actress Jane Froman, portrayed by Susan Hayward in the Academy Award–winning biographical movie, *With a Song in My Heart,* was on a Pan Am flight in 1943 when, during the flight, a woman passenger asked if she would change seats with her. That plane crash-landed near Lisbon, Portugal. Froman nearly lost a leg as a result of the accident, but the woman who took her seat was killed in the crash.

Well-known stuntman Mark Akerstream died during the filming of a staged explosion at sea for the 1998 television series, *The Crow.* Ironically, Akerstream was not in the scene; he was on shore with the rest of the cast and crew. Moments after the explosion, a whistling sound was heard through the trees, followed by a loud thud. They looked down and saw Akerstream lying on the ground. He had been hit in the head by large piece of metal debris.

Two years earlier, Brandon Lee was accidentally killed while filming the original movie version of that television series. The scene
went off as planned: A gun was fired, stage blood squirted, and Lee
collapsed, mortally wounded. It wasn't until the end of the take that
the crew realized Lee wasn't acting. A metal fragment that had become lodged in the prop pistol was discharged by the blanks when
the gun was fired. That fragment fatally wounded the young actor.

In November 2006, Chicago resident Malachi Ritscher set up a video
camera in front of the 25-foot-tall *Flame of the Millennium* sculp-
ture, donned a skull mask, wrapped himself in an American flag,
and climbed onto the base of the monument. In front of him was
a handmade banner reading THOU SHALT NOT KILL. He then lit a match
and set himself on fire.

Earl Metcalfe was a star in the early days of moviemaking. He enlisted
with the famous 165th Infantry Division of the army and was deco-
rated five times for bravery during World War I. After the Armistice,
he resumed his work as an actor, but never achieved the level of success he had attained prior to the war. His final film in 1928 was an

aviation melodrama called *Air Mail Pilot*. The role inspired him to take flying lessons. He fell out of the training airplane and died.

Ettore and Rossana of Padua, Italy, had been married for many years. Ettore faithfully visited his wife in the hospital every day, where she had lain in a coma for several months in 2005 with little hope for recovery. Distraught over the loss of his longtime companion, Ettore committed suicide in the couple's home. Hours later, Rossana woke up.

During the annual Muslim pilgrimage known as the Hajj, the faithful throw rocks at pillars that represent the Devil. It would appear that the Devil retaliates from time to time. In 1997, 340 people died when their tent caught fire.

More often, however, in their eagerness to reach the holy relic or place, the pilgrims just trample each other to death. In 2003, at least fourteen people were crushed under the feet of the impatient crowd in Saudi Arabia. In 2001, thirty-five perished in the same way, and another 180 in 1998.

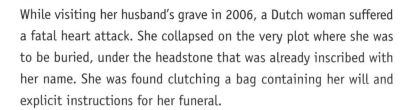

While visiting her husband's grave in 2006, a Dutch woman suffered a fatal heart attack. She collapsed on the very plot where she was to be buried, under the headstone that was already inscribed with her name. She was found clutching a bag containing her will and explicit instructions for her funeral.

Richard "Doc" Brown held a master's degree in biomedical engineering, but was best known as a self-taught and well-respected roller coaster safety expert. He often used himself as a guinea pig to test newly designed rides. In 2005, at the age of 64, he died of head injuries when he slipped and fell in his own driveway.

Yoshiuki Takada was an aerial performer with the Sankai Juku Dance Company of Toyko. In 1985, the troupe performed in Seattle, suspended over the side of the Mutual Life Building. Takada's rope broke and sent him hurtling to the pavement six stories below. The title of Takada's last performance was *The Dance of Birth and Death*.

Summer Lynn Mau and Orem Kauvaka were among a group of fifteen young people who were setting up a roadside marker in Hawaii to serve as a memorial and a warning for reckless drivers. Two of their friends, Pepe Naupoto and Alitha Ah Nee, had been killed in a tragic accident the night before in June 2006. As the mourners stood there, another car plowed into the group and killed Summer and Orem. The following day, the remaining friends set up another marker.

Frank Silvera channeled a rugged handsomeness and commanding stage presence into a successful thirty-year acting career in stage, film, and television. In the years before his death, he appeared in many 1960s television dramas with such colorful titles as *Run for Your Life: The Shock of Recognition* and *The Rat Patrol: The Chain of Death Raid.* He accidentally electrocuted himself while trying to repair a garbage disposal.

Singer-songwriter Bobby Fuller had only one memorable hit in his short career, "I Fought the Law (and the Law Won)" in 1965. A few weeks after the song hit the top of the charts, Fuller's body was found severely beaten and drenched in gasoline, propped up in the front seat of his mother's Oldsmobile. The Los Angeles coroner ruled the death a suicide.

British actor George Sanders won an Academy Award for his role as a snarky theater critic in the film *All About Eve*. He also played the lead in the 1959 movie *Death of a Scoundrel,* and a schoolteacher who takes his own life in *Village of the Damned*. According to the short note found in the room where he died, he killed himself be-cause he was bored.

Lenny Bruce, the famous 1960s satirical stand-up comic and noto-rious drug addict, asked a group of people after a show one night, "Does anybody know where I can get some shit?" He was later found dead of a heroin overdose, sprawled out on the bathroom floor next to his toilet.

In the sixth century BC, the philosopher Chilon of Sparta, who is credited for such words of wisdom as "One must learn how to reg-

Thinning the Herd

ulate one's own house well," and "Nothing in excess," died as the result of an uncontrollable fit of laughter.

A particularly adept Palestinian revolutionary named Yahya Ayyash earned the nickname "The Engineer" for his skill and cunning as a bomb maker. In 1996, he answered a call on his cell phone, which blew up as soon as he pressed the TALK button. The call had come from an airplane flying overhead, which happened to be carrying a few of Yahya's enemies. They were strongly suspected of having booby-trapped Yahya's phone.

In February 2007, archaeologists in Italy discovered the remains of two people buried together more than five thousand years ago. The skeletal remains were entwined in a lovers' embrace. The archaeological dig took place in Mantua, just a few miles south of the hometown of Romeo and Juliet.

Ten minutes into a 1996 performance of *The Makropulos Case* at the Metropolitan Opera in New York City, tenor Richard Versalle fell backward from a 10-foot ladder after singing the line, "You can only live so long."

Versalle fell flat on his back with his arms outstretched, hitting his head on the stage floor below. The fall alone would probably not have killed him. It was the massive heart attack that did him in.

Captain Lawrence Oates was part of the British expedition of 1912, racing to be the first people to reach the South Pole. They became stranded in a deadly blizzard shortly after discovering that a Norwegian team of explorers had already beaten them to the South Pole. On the return trip, a severely frostbitten, starving, and delirious Oates announced to the remaining members of his team, "I am just going outside and may be some time." He was never seen again.

Even if Oates had been able to survive the subfreezing Antarctic climate, it probably would have killed him to know that, just 11 miles away, the Norwegian team had left behind a tent fully stocked with food, fuel, and other supplies. They also left a note wishing Oates and his team good luck in returning home.

Popular British singer Robert Palmer spent a lot of time and energy denying reports of his death in 1997 when a famous music critic by the same name died of liver disease at the age of 52. Not long after the matter seemed finally to be settled, Robert Palmer the singer died of a heart attack at age 54.

For reasons that are sometimes difficult to grasp, Thomas "Stonewall" Jackson was among the most admired military men in American history. A general in the Confederate Army, he was blustery, secretive, controlling, and made terrible decisions regarding the promotion and training of his subordinates—not to mention the fact that he was a leader on the losing side of the Civil War.

Jackson died of injuries sustained during the Battle of Chancellorsville. He was shot multiple times in the shoulder and left arm. During the amputation doctors hoped would save his life, several small round musket balls were removed from Jackson's shoulder, confirming that he had been shot by his own men.

Milton Jacobs was a brilliant chemist, geologist, electrical engineer, physicist, and sailor for the U.S. Navy during World War II. Moments before slipping into the coma from which he would never recover, he said, "I used to know a lot. Now, I don't know nuttin'."

Richard Loeb and Nathan Leopold were childhood friends and sons of privilege with genius-level IQs. Inspired by a story they read in a detective magazine, they set out to commit the perfect crime. In 1924, they kidnapped and brutally murdered a teenage acquaintance, for no other reason than to prove they could get away with it. They did not. Both young men were convicted of murder.

Twelve years later, Loeb was slashed fifty-six times with a razor by a fellow inmate in the Stateville Penitentiary in Joliet, Illinois. As he lay bleeding to death on the shower room floor, he said, "I think I'm going to make it." He did not.

New York City doctor Nicholas Bartha would sooner die than let his money-grubbing, soon-to-be ex-wife make off with half the value of their $6 million Upper East Side townhouse. And so it was. The building collapsed on top of him in the summer of 2006 when he tried to blow it up. The money-grubbing, no-longer-ex-wife, now-widow of the doctor sold the vacant bit of prime real estate for $8.3 million a year later.

Jim Fixx, author of the 1970s best-seller *The Complete Book of Running*, died in 1980 of a heart attack while jogging.

Woodburn Mansion is now the Delaware governor's residence. At one time, it was a stop along the Underground Railroad, a safe haven for black people fleeing to the North in the years before the abolition of slavery.

One particularly vile slave hunter hid in a poplar tree near the mansion, waiting for a runaway slave to sneak onto the property. While sitting on his perch, he accidentally slipped and got his head stuck between two branches of the tree. He hanged by the neck until he died.

Shortly after the publication of Charles Darwin's *The Origin of Species* in 1860, circus and sideshow mogul P. T. Barnum created a new sensation: Zip the Pinhead. Zip was billed as a wild man from Africa, Darwin's missing link between humans and primates. In actuality, Zip was just a guy from New Jersey named William Henry Johnson, who happened to have an oddly shaped head.

The hoax was only one of many in Barnum's big bag of lucrative tricks, but Zip became a shrewd businessman in his own right. After leaving Barnum's sideshow, he went on the road on his own. In a brilliant publicity stunt in 1925, he offered himself up as evidence during the so-called Scopes Monkey Trial, which challenged the teaching of Darwin's *The Origin of Species* in public schools.

Zip the Pinhead died at the age of 66, a very happy and wealthy man. He spoke his last words to his sister: "We sure fooled them, didn't we?"

Pedro Medina was a Cuban refugee convicted and sentenced to die for the stabbing death of a schoolteacher in 1982. If not for the grisly outcome of the execution, he would have quickly faded into obscurity, just another condemned prisoner.

It was the second time in seven years that Florida's electric chair had malfunctioned. Flames a foot high shot from the top of Medina's head. He did die, but not by electrocution; he was roasted alive in that chair.

The last words he spoke were, "I am still innocent."

CHAPTER

5

SO SEXY IT HURTS

Life without sex might be safer, but it
would be unbearably dull.

—Henry Louis Mencken

THE FIRST TIME I let a boy kiss me, I was certain of three things: that
I was pregnant, that what I had done was written all over my face for
all the world to see, and that I was going to go to hell.

I needed to atone, to beg forgiveness for the sake of my immortal
soul and my not-quite-immaculately conceived baby. So I ran all the
way to my grandmother's house, where I ate mangoes all afternoon and

99

said, "Mm-hmm," through a mouthful of fruit to everything she said, even though I had no idea what she was talking about most of the time (she spoke no English). The mangoes, I hoped, would make the funny new feeling on my lips go away, and maybe make me smell like something other than "boy." The visit to my grandmother, who was a very nice lady but a virtual stranger to me at the time, seemed a much more appropriately severe penance than the standard three Hail Marys and an Our Father.

For weeks afterward, I went to church every Saturday and confessed to everything—everything except my one act of depravity. I knew that if I got hit by a bus and died before being officially absolved by a priest, I would spend all of eternity surrounded by other flame-engulfed sinners. But I simply could not bring myself to tell another human being what I had done, not even a priest. Especially not a priest, who was, after all, something allegedly grander than a plain old regular human being.

Of course, I wasn't pregnant, although hell is still a possibility (but that's a story for another day). What was unbearably humiliating to me at that particular moment in my young life was not the "sin" itself, but the fact that other people would know what I had done, and that such knowledge would inevitably bring much pointing and snickering my way.

I wonder if any of the people in the following stories ever pondered a similar fate?

Thinning the Herd

Michael Lord of Massachusetts worshipped his dominatrix, Mistress Lauren M. There was no command he would not obey, no humiliation he would not rapturously endure. During Michael's last visit to Mistress Lauren in the summer of 2000, she strapped all 275 pounds of him to a bondage rack and began to work her magic. Before long, the very happy Michael Lord suffered a fatal heart attack.

Not wanting to draw negative attention to her dominatrix business, Mistress Lauren, whose real name was Barbara Asher, decided against calling 911. Instead, she and her boyfriend and business partner, "Mr. Versace," chopped Michael up into somewhat more manageable pieces, drove north, and dumped him into a large trash bin behind a Chinese restaurant in Maine. Police are still looking for his remains.

In the summer of 2001, Jean-Louis Toubon of Marseilles died while having sex with his girlfriend. He choked to death on her edible panties.

In the summer of 2006, university students Jason Ackerman and Sara Rydman, seeking adventure and a little privacy, crawled inside a deflated helium balloon and got busy. They were found dead of helium poisoning.

Nick Wallis of Oxford, England, was rapidly succumbing to a debilitating neuromuscular disease and was spending his final days in a Catholic assisted-living facility. In 2006, he confided to Sister Frances Dominica, one of the nurses at the facility, that although he had lived a fairly happy life, his one great regret was that he had never had sex. Moved by the young man's plight, the good sister did the compassionate thing. She found him a prostitute on the Internet.

Brandon Sanders of Nashville, Tennessee, told the jurors at his 2006 murder trial that the death of his girlfriend, April Renetta Love, was purely accidental, and he could prove it. He explained how he put a plastic trash bag over her head while they were having sex. Sanders testified that they had done this many times, but nothing had ever gone wrong before.

Thinning the Herd

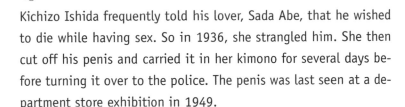

Kichizo Ishida frequently told his lover, Sada Abe, that he wished to die while having sex. So in 1936, she strangled him. She then cut off his penis and carried it in her kimono for several days before turning it over to the police. The penis was last seen at a department store exhibition in 1949.

No one in Richard Pryor's family was particularly surprised when they heard that Richard's father had died while having sex in a brothel. Richard himself had been born in that brothel. His father was the pimp. His mother did double duty as a prostitute and bookkeeper. Grandma was the house madam. Telling the story many years later and marveling over God's benevolence, Pryor said, "My father came—and went—at the same time."

Several popes throughout history were summarily ushered into the next life as a result of their naughty dalliances. Pope John VII was bludgeoned to death by the husband of his mistress when he caught them *in flagrante delicto*. John XIII met his end (so to speak) when a cuckolded husband rammed a poker up his bottom.

Other popes died a bit more privately. Pope Leo VII suffered a fatal heart attack during sex. Pope Paul II was said to have died while being sodomized by a page boy. More recently in history, the short-lived Pope John Paul I, known also as The Smiling Pope and who died just thirty-three days into his papacy, was allegedly so obsessed with pornography that he passed away while "reviewing the literature." (The Vatican is reputed to have one of the largest collections of pornography in the world.)

The body of a man clad in a kinky black leather mask and decked out head to toe in sadomasochistic gear was found hanging from a chain-link fence in Lower Manhattan in September 2006. Untold numbers of New Yorkers walked by and ignored him, assuming the corpse was just an early Halloween display.

In the summer of 2005, Kenneth Pinyan of Seattle, Washington, died of a ruptured colon after he had anal intercourse with a horse. Law enforcement officials did not treat the case as a crime because bestiality was not illegal in Washington State at the time. Also, the horse was unharmed.

Thinning the Herd

Gustav Cleophas Kazandu, a teenager from the town of Grootfontein in Namibia, found a curiously shaped object one day in 2007, but wasn't sure what it was. He took it to his uncle to see if he could identify it. The uncle told him it looked like the shriveled penis of an old man, so the two concluded it was either a sex toy or an educational aid. The young man took the object to school to show his friends. The penis exploded, killing Gustav and one of his friends, and injuring five others. As it turns out, the object was a grenade.

In 1899, the president of France, Félix Faure, died while receiving oral gratification from his mistress. When the woman became aware that the president had become "unusually stiff," she panicked and began to scream. The president's aides broke down the door when they heard the muffled cries. They found Faure seated on a sofa, with his mistress kneeling before him.

Separating the lovers turned out to be a rather complicated task. Faure died with the woman's long black hair clutched in his hands in a death grip. Further, the shock of realizing what had just happened to her caused the woman to suffer trauma-induced lockjaw. They did eventually free the hysterical woman from her lover's crotch, but doctors had to pry Faure's member from her clenched mouth.

The aides were later credited for having had the presence of mind to put their fallen leader in a more dignified pose before taking the woman to the hospital. The next day's newspapers showed a photograph of Faure lying in bed with his hands neatly folded over a crucifix.

Anthony Casey fell 60 feet from a balcony to his death during a drug-fueled gay orgy in London in 2006, in an apartment owned by Count Gottfried von Bismarck. The coroner listed the cause of death as "Misadventure."

In 1975, American cartoonist Vaughn Bodé accidentally suffocated while having sex with himself. Some reports of his death indicate that he was riding a motorcycle at the time.

Albert Dekker, star of the 1940 movie *Dr. Cyclops,* was found hanging from a shower curtain rod, with dirty hypodermic needles in each arm, wearing women's lingerie, and obscenities written in

Thinning the Herd

lipstick all over his body. Not quite sure what to make of the scene, officials ruled that the death of the 62-year-old actor was "accidental suicide"—a series of autoerotic escapades gone slightly haywire.

St. Louis weatherman Bob Richards of KDSK-TV deliberately crashed his own small plane in 1994 after being publicly humiliated on a local morning radio show. The relentlessly puerile hosts of the show, Steve and DC, thought it would be hugely entertaining to play audiotapes of Richards's sexy telephone conversations with his mistress on the air. The DJs were fired, but Richards was already dead.

In 1990, actor William Gardner Knight was on his way to a party scheduled to take place on board a friend's boat anchored near Annapolis, Maryland. Anticipating a fun-filled evening, Knight got into his private plane, popped some Viagra, and headed toward Maryland. He overshot the landing strip at Lee Airport, crashed into murky Beard's Creek, and died in the wreckage. It turns out that, in a small number of people, Viagra causes temporary color blindness, which is a bad thing for a night-flying pilot.

Grigory Rasputin, known also as "The Mad Monk," was a trusted friend of the Romanovs, Russia's last royal family. Rasputin inspired more fear, awe, and envy, however, for the size of his penis than for his connections to the throne. Rasputin's foot-long member was festooned with an enormous wart, located in just such a position as to cause some of his lovers to lose consciousness.

After his death in 1916, Rasputin's penis became a collector's item. In 1995, someone claiming to be the rightful owner arranged to have it sold at auction at Christie's. The item was withdrawn, however, when investigators discovered that it was a sea cucumber, not a penis. The genuine article is currently on display at the Erotic Museum in St. Petersburg, which also operates as a prostate clinic under the direction of Dr. Igor Knyazkin.

Another famously deceased penis was the one once attached to Napoleon Bonaparte. It was severed at his autopsy, then stolen shortly thereafter. It resurfaced some years later and was purchased by an American urologist for $40,000 in 1977. In comparing this specimen to Rasputin's, Dr. Knyazkin described Napoleon's little friend as, "but a small pod."

Reports of "penis snatching" are fairly common in West Africa. There is a belief that a man's genitalia will shrivel, fall off, or disappear if he so much as shakes hands with a sorcerer. Some men have claimed to be sorcerers, only to extort money in exchange for a "cure." At least seven such con artists were beaten to death by angry mobs in Ghana in 1997.

Silent movie star Ramon Novarro was one of the most handsome and admired actors of his time. He did make it into the talkies, but his star quickly waned and he fell into relative obscurity during his final years. On Halloween night in 1968, two assailants broke into his home and bludgeoned him to death with one of Novarro's most cherished possessions: an Art Deco dildo given to him by his friend, Rudolph Valentino.

Brocket Hall in Hertfordshire, England, is rife with stories of the sexual exploits of its past residents. Lady Caroline Lamb once arranged herself inside a large soup tureen and had the servants serve her naked to her lover, Lord Byron. The elderly yet spry prime minister Lord Palmerston died happily on his own billiard table after helping himself to a young parlor maid. Brocket Hall is now a successful conference center, very popular with the corporate folk.

The ancient custom of *minghun* is still alive and well in certain remote regions of China. It involves burying a "ghost bride" (a recently deceased woman) with a dead bachelor, so that he won't be lonely in the afterlife.

The enterprising pimping team of Yang Dongyan and Liu Shenghai figured out that they could get more money for a dead woman than a live prostitute, so they went into business with an undertaker. In 2006, Chinese police arrested all three men for murdering young women for the purpose of selling them as ghost brides.

An unidentified couple in Bucharest was found dead, post-coitus, in their car. They had, apparently, forgotten the most important safety rule for having sex in the backseat of a car: Either turn off the ignition or open the garage door.

A 65-year-old German retiree living in Costa del Sol, Spain, was the proud inventor of a homemade sex toy. He rigged a voltmeter in such a way that he could apply the electrodes to his genitalia to give himself an extra little buzz. In 2003, he popped a porn tape into the VCR and flipped the switch on his new toy. He was found sometime later, still wired, dead of a heart attack.

❧

Silent film star Virginia Rappe died of massive internal injuries after having sex with the 300-pound comic actor Roscoe "Fatty" Arbuckle. After three sensational trials, Fatty was cleared of any wrongdoing, but he never worked in Hollywood again. He just wasn't so funny anymore after that.

❧

Bryan Hathaway argued that he could not be criminally prosecuted for having sex with a deer because the animal was dead at the time. His lawyer further explained that the deer "ceased being an animal upon its death." Hathaway was ordered to stand trial anyway, not for his sexual encounter with the animal—dead or alive—but because sexual immorality is illegal in Wisconsin.

❧

Mervin Touchet, second Earl of Castlehaven, was executed in 1631 on two counts of sodomy and one of abetting rape. If he had been allowed to plead innocent because he was clergy, he might have been exonerated, as many other clerics of the day had been lucky enough to do. Instead, he got the guillotine.

In 2004, a 68-year-old mother from Seville, Spain, was horrified to find her 45-year-old bachelor son having sex with a blow-up doll. She destroyed the offensive object by popping it with a pin. The man responded by stabbing his mother sixty-one times.

Stanford White was a millionaire architect in early-twentieth-century New York. In 1906, while standing near the top of the original Madison Square Garden, which he himself had designed, Stanford was shot and killed by Harry Thaw. The great love of Stanford's life, Evelyn Nesbit, witnessed the murder. Evelyn was Harry's wife.

Zhou Jingzhi thought he had come up with a uniquely satisfying way of mending his broken heart and restoring his honor as a man: He forcibly tattooed insults on the bodies of women who had re-

Thinning the Herd

jected him as a lover. The Chinese government was not pleased. Zhou Jingzhi was sentenced to death for his crime.

General David Bradford was a slave owner in St. Francisville, Louisiana, in the late 1700s. He had a particularly curious slave named Chloe, and a horny son-in-law named Clarke Woodruff. It was rumored that Chloe was Woodruff's concubine, and that she had heard through the grapevine that Woodruff was eyeing a new bedmate. Woodruff caught Chloe eavesdropping on him, and cut off her ear to cure her of that unpleasant habit. Chloe made amends by baking a special birthday cake for his daughter, flavored with the aromatic leaves of the oleander tree. Woodruff's wife and both daughters died of oleander poisoning.

In 2005, carpenter William Goss from the city of Jersey in England failed to see the humor in his fiancée's little jibes. She thought it enormously witty to tell people that the only thing he was good for was being her sex slave. Having heard the joke once too often, Goss killed her in a fit of rage. He then fled to France, but turned himself in two days later.

Many a young man in search of fortune in the early 1900s ended up in Canada's Yukon Territory during the days of gold-rush fever. One in particular did strike it rich, and immediately sent for his fiancée. Young Mary checked into a hotel in Skagway, Alaska, and waited for her true love. She waited a very long time. Mary was found lying on her hotel bed, emaciated, and dressed in her wedding gown.

Legendary womanizer Giacomo Casanova once boasted of having bested the ultimate jealous husband—God himself—when a gorgeous yet duplicitous nun passed him a note one day and invited him into her bed. It was an invitation extended many times by the naughty nun, and accepted just as often by the lascivious Casanova.

Casanova died in the Castle of Dux in Bohemia in 1798, a lonely old man. He was despised and shunned by nearly everyone, including the servants. His last words, spoken to Prince de Ligne, were as ironic as they were magnificently self-deceiving: "I have lived as a philosopher, and die as a Christian."

When he wasn't in jail or in a pub, beloved bad boy Brendan Behan wrote plays and stories full of biting wit, heart-wrenching tragedy, and brilliant humor. A difficult childhood in the slums of Ireland laid the groundwork for the troubled life yet to come, but from the worst experiences came his best work. As he lay dying in a Catholic hospital in 1964, the victim of his own indulgences and reckless living, a nurse came to take his pulse. He turned toward the nun and said, "Bless you, Sister. May all your sons be bishops."

CHAPTER

6

RAMPAGE OF ANGELS

EVERY NORMAL MAN MUST BE TEMPTED AT TIMES

TO SPIT UPON HIS HANDS, HOIST THE BLACK FLAG,

AND BEGIN SLITTING THROATS.

—Lucanus (AD 39–65)

ANGRY, OUT-OF-CONTROL, raging people scare me. I have a very long fuse, myself. Eventually, of course, it runs out, but it can take years before I realize that something is really bothering me.

Occasionally, however, I'll come across one of those people, like a coworker or an ex-husband, who just happens to be very good at tweaking that one little raw nerve for which I haven't yet had enough years of psychotherapy. A little tweak here, a little twang there, until finally something . . . just . . . snaps. And then, all of a sudden—like a miracle—I understand with absolute, crystalline clarity how an otherwise well-liked, intelligent, endlessly calm and patient human being can arrive at the notion that climbing a tower with an automatic weapon and several rounds of ammunition is a perfectly appropriate response to any annoying situation.

Then the moment passes and I find a few more inches of fuse. And that's a good thing, too, because nobody scares me more than me with no more fuse left.

Would that we all could always find a few more inches of fuse. But of course, some of us don't.

Katherine Knight of Aberdeen, Australia, was appalled to hear that she would have to spend the rest of her life in prison. She maintained that her crime hadn't been *that* bad. In February of 2000, the 50-year-old butcher stabbed her live-in boyfriend, John Price, thirty-seven times. She then skinned him, cut him up into slabs, and hung his various parts on meat hooks in the living room of the house they had shared. Furthermore, even though Katherine wasn't particularly fond of the man's now-adult children, she invited them over for dinner anyway. She served them a nice stew of potatoes, vegetables, their father's boiled head, and filet of baked butt-cheeks with brown gravy.

On a rural road in the mountain region of Pantelhó, Mexico, in 2006, an argument broke out between two families over who was responsible for repairing a pothole. The dispute ended in gunfire, with four people dead, three others injured, and the pothole still unrepaired.

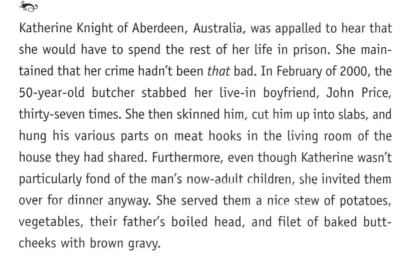

In the early 1500s, Martin Luther broke from the Catholic Church and began what history would record as the Protestant Reformation.

Five hundred years later, in November 2006, a Lutheran vicar named Roland Weisselberg visited the Erfurt monastery, where Martin Luther took his monastic vows. Weisselberg doused himself in gasoline, lit a match, and torched himself. In a letter he left for his wife, Weisselberg expressed his outrage over the "Islamization" of Europe and the dangers of religious fanaticism.

Suresh Kumar, a 25-year-old tailor from Bangalore, India, doused himself in gasoline and lit himself on fire in protest of the 1996 Miss World beauty pageant. Before lighting the match, Kumar shouted slogans criticizing the pageant's exploitation of women. His last words were reportedly, "Water! Water! Water!"

Clara Harris of Texas was forced to recant her initial claim that the death of her husband was an accident. She had been caught on tape in 2002 behind the wheel of her Mercedes-Benz, running him over—and over and over—in the parking lot of a Houston hotel. Clara had followed her husband and his mistress into the lobby of the hotel, where all three were promptly thrown out by guards when the loud confrontation between the wife, the husband, and

Thinning the Herd

his lover turned into a fistfight. All of this occurred in the very hotel in which Mr. and Mrs. Harris had celebrated their wedding reception a decade earlier.

Jean-Paul Marat was a French revolutionary with a profound hatred of the rich and powerful. Through his often-banned periodical *L'ami du peuple* ("The Friend of the People"), which he filled with bitter rants against the monarchy and other members of the elite, Marat became the de facto leader of a group that called itself the *Sans-Culottes* ("Those with No Pants" or "the Bare-Assed).

Marat spent a lot of time in a tub of cold water for relief of his herpes-like skin disease. Thusly immersed, he often indulged in one of his favorite pastimes: adding new names to his "death list," a detailed inventory of his enemies. While Marat was sitting in his tub one fine summer day in 1793, Charlotte Corday, posing as a messenger in need of his help, entered his chambers. He asked the woman for the names of the people who had wronged her, and diligently added them to his list. "They shall all be guillotined," he said as he wrote, at which point Charlotte pulled out a knife and stabbed him to death.

Marat's bathtub was stolen by members of the very same wealthy elite he so hated. The tub changed hands many times over the next hundred years, a coveted collectors' item.

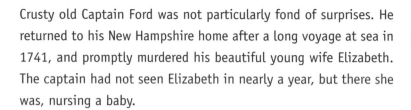

Crusty old Captain Ford was not particularly fond of surprises. He returned to his New Hampshire home after a long voyage at sea in 1741, and promptly murdered his beautiful young wife Elizabeth. The captain had not seen Elizabeth in nearly a year, but there she was, nursing a baby.

Carl Panzram of Minnesota began his career as a serial killer at the age of 8. Later in life he added "nomad" to his list of skills, and slaughtered people on nearly every continent on the planet. While in Africa, he once killed six men in a single day and fed their bodies to the crocodiles. He was finally captured and sentenced to death by hanging in 1930. On the day of his execution, Panzram ran gleefully up the steps of the Leavenworth Penitentiary's gallows, spat in his executioner's face, and yelled, "Hurry up, you bastard! I could've killed ten men while you're fooling around here!"

In October 2006, Kevin Harville drove down a California highway at 65 miles per hour, aiming for the back of his girlfriend's car. Instead of rear-ending her, Harville lost control of his own car and rolled it over. The battery popped out and crashed through the windshield of another car. Shawn Kettlewell, who had nothing to do with Harville's relationship woes, died instantly. Harville and his girlfriend survived.

The American-appointed mayor of Sadr City became incensed when soldiers dared to insist that he follow security checkpoint procedures in Baghdad in November 2003. He got into a heated argument with an American soldier and wrestled him to the ground. The soldier's rifle accidentally discharged, shooting the mayor in the thigh. The mayor was immediately transported to a U.S. military hospital, where he was pronounced dead on arrival.

In 1905, in a rage over not being able to remember the combination code to the safe in his office, Jack Daniel, founder of the famous Tennessee whiskey distillery, kicked the safe and broke his toe. He died of blood poisoning a few days later.

While attending a wedding in Cancún, Mexico, in 2007, a British couple got into a bit of a spat on the balcony of their fourteenth-floor luxury hotel room. Adrian Fletcher and his girlfriend Lisa Miller began arguing after an all-night drinking session in the hotel lobby. At one point, Fletcher picked up his girlfriend and threw her off the balcony, but he fell with her. Fortunately, they both landed on the balcony of the floor just below them. When hotel security guards burst onto the scene, Fletcher spread his arms like some kind of giant bird, smiled, and took a dive over the railing, aiming for the swimming pool below. Even if he had hit the water, it is unlikely that he would have survived the fall. As it happened, he landed on the concrete deck.

Amish teenager Danny Crawford was out having a little old-fashioned fun with some friends in December 2006. They were tossing tomatoes at passing cars. Danny was shot to death by an irate motorist who didn't think it was that funny.

James French was found guilty of killing a motorist in 1958 and was sentenced to life in prison. Disappointed that he was not to be ex-

Thinning the Herd

ecuted, and unable to kill himself despite several tries, French took another approach: He strangled his cellmate to death. At last, French got his wish. Strapped into Oklahoma's electric chair in 1966, he turned to witnesses and reporters and said, "How's this for tomorrow's headline? *FRENCH FRIES!*"

The prescription sleep aid Halcion was banned in the United States and Britain in the early 1990s after numerous reports of adverse side effects, including mild amnesia and disorientation. The ban came a little too late for Mildred Coates. The 83-year-old Iowa woman was found by police, stretched out on her bed, clutching a cheery birthday card in her left hand, and with her brains splattered across her pillow. Her daughter, 63-year-old insomniac Ilo Grundberg, had no clear recollection of having shot her mother nine times in the head.

In January 2007, a man from the Karelia region of Russia stabbed and bludgeoned his 81-year-old grandmother to death when they could not agree on what program to watch on television. In court, the man's lawyer said his client was drunk at the time and could not remember exactly what it was he had wanted to watch.

In 2000, Jonathan Burton of Las Vegas, Nevada, attempted to storm the cockpit during a Southwest Airlines flight from Phoenix to Salt Lake City. Other passengers immediately stepped in to stop the out-of-control teenager. He was in such a rage that some of the passengers began beating him. When that failed to subdue him, they piled on top of him. Burton finally quieted down. He was smothered to death.

Immigration lawyer Richard Baumhammers went on a homicidal rampage in his suburban Pittsburgh, Pennsylvania, neighborhood in April of 2000. Baumhammers drove his Jeep from house to house, killing five people he had singled out for their race or ethnicity. His attorney explained that the rampage was merely an outward expression of Baumhammers's belief that he was being watched by the FBI, that his maid was a spy, and that his skin was falling off.

To better exert their authority, or perhaps for their own protection, health officials in China often travel in very large groups. In July

2001, fifty meat inspectors paid a visit to Guan Jiadong's butcher shop. Citing serious health hazards, they began to confiscate the meat. Guan Jiadong grabbed a bunch of his knives, hopped on his motorbike, and plowed straight into the group. He hacked four of the inspectors to death right where they stood. He also managed to carve a few large chunks out of three other men before he was finally subdued.

Ryuji Sakamoto had held his tongue for as long as he could. He simply could not fathom why his friend Takayuki Niimi persisted in his refusal to address Mr. Sakamoto using the respectful honorific "san" after his first name. Then one day in 2002, he snapped. He punched Niimi in the face several times, knocked him to the floor, and stabbed him in the head with his umbrella. Interestingly, Niimi was the second person to be stabbed in the head with an umbrella in Japan that month.

The 2003 ban on smoking in New York City bars and restaurants did little to prolong the life of one East Village nightclub bouncer. Dana Blake, a 6-foot-5 wall of a man known to his friends as

Shazam, was stabbed to death by an angry bar patron who had been asked to put out his cigarette.

A 59-year-old Dutch man was fed up with the way the Philips electronics company was peddling its wide-screen television sets, which he considered to be inferior in quality. So he went to the Rembrandt Tower in downtown Amsterdam and took eighteen employees hostage at gunpoint. What he had not realized was that Philips had moved to the building next door the year before, in 2001. Seven hours into the siege, the hostage-taker went into the men's room and shot himself in the head. The first bullet didn't kill him, so he shot himself again. Police later described the man as "confused."

Lloyd Robert Jeffress took an AK-47 and a sawed-off .22-caliber rifle into a Benedictine monastery in rural Missouri and shot the priest who greeted him at the door. He also shot a Brother who was tending the garden. Monks all over the monastery ran away in terror and hid in their rooms. Jeffress wandered the halls of the monastery's business offices and shot a few more people, and then went to sit in the chapel for a while. The last shot he fired was into his own head. Jeffress's ex-wife later told police that he'd been very angry over their divorce. Their marriage had ended forty-three years earlier.

If there was one thing 56-year-old Franklin Crow hated, it was finding out too late that the toilet paper roll was empty. Franklin had spoken to his roommate Kenneth Matthews about this many times, reminding him over and over that it was simply common courtesy to replace the roll. The last time Franklin spoke to Kenny about this, in February 2006, he did so with a mallet in one hand and a claw hammer in the other. The only identifiable part of Kenneth Matthews that remained after this discussion was his fingerprints.

The adage "Marry in haste, repent at leisure" was never truer than for accused murderer Brandon Manai. Shortly after a quickie wedding in Las Vegas in the summer of 2005, Manai and his new bride, Julia Rosas, returned to their respective parents' homes. Julia did not care for Brandon's possessiveness, so she asked him for a divorce. Brandon was accused of inviting her to come with him to the nearby Los Angeles hills, where he threw her off a 200-foot cliff. If convicted, Manai will have plenty of time to repent in jail.

In 2006, a severe winter storm kept temperatures in the twenties and thousands of homes in St. Louis, Missouri, without power for several days. It was perhaps a combination of cabin fever and alcohol that led one woman to shoot her 70-year-old husband to death in the kitchen of their home after he gave her a can of warm beer. It had occurred to neither one of them to chill a six-pack on the back porch.

A 2006 marital dispute in Hamilton Heights, New York, turned tragic when Donna Cobbs beat her husband Kevin with a ceramic elephant. When he collapsed, Donna tried to resuscitate him by giving him CPR. Kevin died at Harlem Hospital, where Donna worked as a nurse.

Ricky Vega of Tyler, Texas, was determined to succeed on his second attempt to win a brand new 2005 Nissan truck in a local dealership's annual contest. A family emergency had caused him to drop out of the competition the previous year. This time, he was going to keep his hand on the truck for as long as it took, until he was declared the last person standing. Three days into the contest, Vega took his hand off the truck, calmly walked across the street, and threw a trash can through a Kmart window. He retrieved a shotgun from the back of the store, walked outside, and blew his brains out.

Marc Lépine will probably go down in history as Canada's worst mass murderer. He went on a shooting spree in 1989 at a technical college in Montreal, shouting, "I hate feminists!" He killed fourteen women before turning the gun on himself. The dealer who sold Lépine the gun later said of the disturbed young man, "He didn't appear any crazier than anybody else."

No one felt particularly compelled to render aid to suspected serial killer Moninder Singh Pandher, not even his own attorneys. At Pandher's arraignment in January 2007, lawyers from both sides of the table, court officers, and even the judge dragged Pandher into the streets and kicked him all the way to the district court police station. They punched him, kneed him in the groin, and pulled the hairs out of his moustache. They also yanked his pants off. Some lawyers stood on top of parked cars and led the frenzied crowds of spectators in chanting, "Kill the cannibal!" Pandher, who was charged with the gruesome murders of at least twenty-one people, was turned in by his own servant, a man curiously named Surendra.

A protest over the food on board the RMS *Queen Mary* during World War II escalated into a riot. American troops being transported across the Atlantic had become increasingly dissatisfied with the cook's disgusting concoctions, which only became less edible with each passing day. Unable to take it anymore, the rioters beat the man senseless, stuffed him into his own oven, and baked him to death.

If the diminutive Italian immigrant Giuseppe Zangara had been as good a marksman as he was a bricklayer, he might have hit his target, president-elect Franklin D. Roosevelt. Instead, he killed Anton Cermak, the mayor of Chicago. Zangara, nonetheless, paid quickly for his crime. In 1933, in a matter of thirty-three days, he

Thinning the Herd

was arrested, tried, found guilty, and sentenced to die in the electric chair.

Standing defiantly in front of Old Sparky, Zangara proceeded to deliver one of history's most memorable good-bye speeches: "You give me electric chair. I no afraid of that chair! You one of capitalists! You is crook man, too! Put me in electric chair! I no care!" When a minister tried to calm him, Zangara said to him, "Get to hell out of here, you son of a bitch!" and resumed his parting speech. "I go sit down all by myself . . . Viva Italia! Good-bye to all poor peoples everywhere! Lousy capitalists! No picture! No one here to take my picture! All capitalists lousy bunch of crooks! Go ahead! Pusha da button!"

And so they did.

In the 1040s, a young Kentucky woman named Melissa fell in love with her tutor, a Bostonian named William Beverleigh. Alas, Melissa's love was unrequited; he was in love with her neighbor. Consumed by jealousy, Melissa devised a plan. She lured her teacher deep inside nearby Mammoth Cave, the largest known cavern in the world. She took him to a spot called Purgatory Point, then snuck away and left him to find his own way out. No one ever saw that damned Yankee again.

The sadistic captain of the USF *Constellation*, Thomas Truxtun, ordered the execution of a young sailor named Neil Harvey in 1799. Harvey had committed the unforgivable offense of falling asleep while on duty. The captain ordered that Harvey be strapped to one of the ship's cannons. Harvey was blown to bits when the captain yelled, "Fire!"

In 1827, Joseph Smith found a holy book on a hill near his home in Palmyra, New York, and founded the Mormon religion. He managed to organize a rather large group of followers over the coming years, but learned soon enough that great power often breeds great enemies. By the spring of 1844, a number of prominent Mormons in Illinois, where Smith was then living, set out to expose Smith as a fraud based on rumors of polygamy, strange sexual liaisons, and other unorthodox practices. Smith responded by ordering the destruction of the free press. Satisfied that Smith had sealed his own fate and proven himself to be a theocratic tyrant, the dissidents murdered him in his own jail cell, where Smith had hoped to hide from the angry mob until the kerfuffle blew over. Brigham Young gathered up the remaining followers and fled Illinois. They didn't stop until they got to Utah.

Thinning the Herd

During the Civil War, an abolitionist from Kansas named John Brown led a group of men to Harpers Ferry, West Virginia. Their plan was to break into the Confederate Arsenal and steal guns to arm themselves and the slaves. Ninety marines under the command of General Robert E. Lee captured Brown and his men before they could complete the mission. Brown was hanged, and one of his men was chopped up and fed to the pigs.

Barbara Graham and two accomplices were convicted of beating and strangling a handicapped widow in Burbank, California, in 1955. Graham was sentenced to die in the gas chamber at the San Quentin penitentiary. As the executioner escorted her into the chamber, he said, "Now take a deep breath and it won't bother you." Barbara looked at him sideways and replied, "How in the hell would you know?!"

A 57-year-old Bulgarian woman in the last stages of terminal cancer was granted a "mercy release" from prison. She had been serving time for killing her own son with a garden hoe in 2005 while he was sleeping. As soon as she got home, she stabbed her husband in the throat. He died. The woman was immediately taken back into custody, but promised that, if released, she would kill her other son.

7

IT SEEMED LIKE
A GOOD IDEA AT
THE TIME

IN VIEW OF THE FACT THAT GOD LIMITED THE INTELLIGENCE OF MAN,
IT SEEMS UNFAIR THAT HE DID NOT ALSO LIMIT HIS STUPIDITY.

—Konrad Adenauer (1876–1967)

ONE UNUSUALLY COLD evening in Atlanta in the winter of 1985, I was driving my little tin can of a car home from the university where I was taking a few classes. Waiting for the light to change, happy that the heater was working, and feeling smugly certain that I had just turned in yet another A+ paper, I felt the guy in the car behind me hit my rear bumper. Just a tap, no big deal. So, of course, I made a big deal out of it.

I made a great show of getting out of my car, slamming the door indignantly, and meticulously inspecting my already decrepit bumper. I even sneered at the poor schmuck sitting behind the wheel of his evil yuppie Beemer as he sat there looking at me like I was crazy. Satisfied that no damage had been done, I walked back toward the front of my car and, to my absolute horror, found that all the doors were locked. I had an eighth of a tank of gas left, the engine and heater were running, and the headlights were on. Also, I was in my stocking feet. I could see my keys, my bag, and my shoes inside the car. So close . . . so far. So I did the only thing I could do in that moment. I walked back over to the yuppie, motioned for him to roll down the window, and said, "You don't happen to have a coat hanger in there, do you?"

In that instant, one of life's great truths became crystal clear to me: At any given moment in time, somebody has to be the stupidest person in the world. I believe wholeheartedly that that's a provable mathematical fact. That day, in that moment, it was my turn.

We all get a turn at some point in our lives. Most of us will live to pass the baton on to the next hapless moron-du-jour. Some of us, alas, do not.

Thinning the Herd

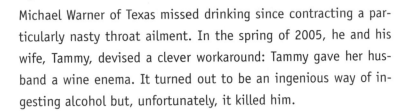

Michael Warner of Texas missed drinking since contracting a particularly nasty throat ailment. In the spring of 2005, he and his wife, Tammy, devised a clever workaround: Tammy gave her husband a wine enema. It turned out to be an ingenious way of ingesting alcohol but, unfortunately, it killed him.

The wife of popular radio talk-show host and former sports broadcaster Vince Marinello was killed near their home in New Orleans. Marinello told police he was in Mississippi at the time. If not for one minor oversight, the well-known personality might actually have gotten away with it. On the last day of his wife's life, Marinello disguised himself as a bum and rode a bicycle to a place where he knew she had an appointment. Once there, he shot her twice in the face, and rode away. Police searched Marinello's home and found a list in his handwriting. Some of the items on the list were, "Bicycle, costume, gun."

An old World War II bomb blew up and killed a fisherman off the coast of Tirana, Albania, in July of 1996. The man had intended to detonate the bomb in the ocean to facilitate catching massive amounts of fish at once. Although it is illegal in Albania to kill fish with explosives, many fishermen continue to make use of the numerous old bombs that still litter the coast. Dead and dismembered fishermen are also numerous in this part of the world.

Charles G. Stephens thought he had figured out why so many people had killed themselves going over Niagara Falls in a barrel: they didn't use a counterweight. So in the summer of 1920, Charles outfitted his wooden barrel with an anvil, got inside, and strapped himself in. The only part of Charles G. Stevens that was ever found was his right arm, still inside the barrel.

In 1753, Professor Georg Richmann of St. Petersburg, Russia, wanted to test the effects of lightning during a thunderstorm. He attached a wire to the top of his house and connected it to a device made up of an insulated rod and an iron bar suspended above a bowl filled with water and brass fillings. As Richmann and his assistant observed the approach of a distant storm, a ball of lightning suddenly bounced off the rod and smacked Richmann on the forehead. Richmann's shoes were blown apart, his clothes were singed, the doorframe was split open, and the door was torn off its hinges. Richmann looked remarkably peaceful despite the fact that he was lying flat on his back, quite dead. His wife saw him and thought he was napping, so she left him there. His assistant woke up after a brief moment of unconsciousness. Except for a few scattered pellets, the contraption was utterly undisturbed.

The HMS *Curacao* was one of several smaller ships escorting the massive *Queen Mary* luxury liner in the North Atlantic during World War II. The spunky little *Curacao* cut in front of the 81,000-ton *Queen Mary* and was sliced right through the middle. Too bad it was wartime, too. Otherwise, the *Queen Mary* might have been allowed to stop and save some of the 439 men that were hurled into the water. Only 101 of them survived.

Robert Chalmers went mad in 1879, which made him wickedly violent. For his own protection—but probably more for her own—his wife Louisa chained him to a pipe in the basement of their Coloma,

California, house. Robert eventually quieted down. He became convinced his wife was trying to poison him, so he stopped eating. Chalmers starved to death.

The widow of a U.S. marine thought she had planned the perfect murder. Cynthia Sommer slowly poisoned her husband to collect $250,000 in veterans' benefits. She used the money for better clothes, parties, and a boob job.

In an effort to simultaneously cover her tracks and appear noble in her new role as the widow of a war hero, she donated Todd Sommer's organs to a local hospital upon his death in February 2002. She had the rest of him cremated. Lab tests on the donated organs revealed hundreds of times the normal level of arsenic in his liver and kidneys. Cynthia was, as they say, busted.

Several thatch-walled shelters were set up in Southern India to house the mentally ill, where patients were chained to poles. Doctors rarely, if ever, visited the shelters. Instead, the huts were placed near an 800-year-old Muslim shrine with the expectation that the patients would be cured via miraculous intervention.

Fifteen of the Erwadi shelters were closed and fifty inmates freed after a fire broke out in one of the huts in 2001. The fire killed twenty-eight of the shackled patients. No one in the vicinity called the fire department because they thought there was nothing unusual at all about all the screaming inside the hut.

In January 2006, David Galvan and his uncle Rafael Vargas were having a good time drinking in their home in Barranquilla, Colombia. At some point during the evening, Galvan was overcome by a terrible bout of the hiccups. Vargas knew the perfect cure for this malady: He pointed a gun at his nephew. The hiccups stopped immediately after the gun went off. Horrified over the accidental killing, Vargas then turned the gun on himself.

For some musicians, the bathroom is the most dangerous place in the world. Keith Relf of The Yardbirds was electrocuted in his London home while tuning his guitar in 1976; he was taking a bath at the time. Claude François, a French pop singer, electrocuted himself in 1978 when he tried to fix a broken lightbulb while standing in his bathtub.

Acting on a tip, police arrived at the Dyckman Houses in Upper Manhattan in 2001 to arrest two men suspected of gaining illegal access to a public housing apartment. As they approached the building, a pair of hands inside a plastic bag was tossed from a window and landed at their feet. Once upstairs, the officers found a hacksaw and a bathtub filled with bloody water. They also found a severed head under the kitchen sink.

Bernard Perez was arrested at the scene, as was his accomplice, Rahman Williams. It was not the first time Perez had scored an apartment in New York City's brutally competitive housing market by killing the former occupants. Amazingly, Perez was out on parole despite having admitted his participation in a similar apartment-snatching scheme. If the hog-tied body of Doris Drakeford had not finally floated to the surface of the Harlem River, Perez might still be living in her apartment; her rent was paid automatically through her welfare benefits.

At a Christmas party in Aurora, Colorado, in 2000, Manuel Dominguez-Quintero dared his friend to shoot a plastic drinking cup off his head with a .25-caliber semiautomatic pistol. William

Tell he was not. The bullet went directly into Manuel's head. The plastic cup was untouched.

Lusaed Perez of Yonkers, New York, always took great pride in her appearance. While applying makeup one morning in 2006, she drove her Mitsubishi head-on into a stand of trees along the Henry Hudson Parkway. After they removed her body from the scene of the accident, a police officer told a reporter, "There was makeup all over the air bag."

In August 2006, the owner of a tree service in Pleasant Prairie, Wisconsin, was sucked into his own wood chipper and spat out the other end in little bitty pieces. The wood chipper had become clogged with a loose piece of wood, so he kicked it a few times to dislodge it. The chipper roared back to life. The gardener did not.

A man fleeing police in Tijuana, Mexico, lost control of his motorcycle and crashed in October 2005. He was able to elude authorities by running into the brush that grew along the highway. He left behind his passenger, a corpse in a helmet. Police believed the motorcyclist had killed the man earlier in the day and was looking for a place to dump the body. The helmet was used to make the corpse appear less conspicuous.

Christian Ponce became yet one more killer in a long line of elusive criminals who were captured for reasons that had nothing to do with their crimes. Ponce was wanted in Ecuador in connection with the 1999 assassination of a former presidential candidate and his bodyguard. Seven years later, while driving along a country road outside Buffalo, New York, he was stopped for driving without a seat belt.

Other criminals who wished they had taken a bus more often include serial killers Ted Bundy, David "Son of Sam" Berkowitz, and Henry Lee Lucas.

The steady, cool climate inside of Mammoth Cave in Kentucky seemed the perfect healing environment for people suffering from

Thinning the Herd

tuberculosis. Louisville physician John Croghan set up a clinic inside the cave and moved eleven of his patients there in 1842. They all got worse immediately. Some died in the cave. The rest died shortly after Croghan moved them back into a real hospital. Then Croghan died, too.

The most famous passenger on board a 1948 United Airlines flight was theatrical impresario Earl Carroll. During the flight, a fire broke out in the cargo hold at the rear of the plane. The flight crew immediately set about the task of putting it out with a fire extinguisher. The pilot and copilot were soon incapacitated by the carbon dioxide emitted from the extinguisher, leaving the plane to crash on its own.

Derek Kieper, an intensely vocal opponent of the seat-belt laws he considered "intrusions on civil liberties and expensive to enforce," died in 2004 when he was ejected from a Ford Explorer that skidded off an icy section of Interstate 80 in Nebraska. The driver and two other passengers, who were wearing seat belts, survived.

Stuntman A. J. Bakunas made it into the *Guinness Book of World Records* for performing the highest movie stunt jump without a parachute. During the filming of the 1997 movie *Steel,* he successfully performed a fall from the ninth floor of a construction site in Lexington, Kentucky. When he learned that Dar Robinson, another stuntman, had broken his record high-fall, Bakunas repeated the stunt, but this time from the top of the 300-foot construction site. Bakunas executed the jump expertly, but the air bag he landed on exploded. Bakunas died on impact.

Teenage beauty queen Tara Rose McAvoy of Texas was busy text-messaging family and friends on her cell phone in 2006 while walking along the Union Pacific railroad tracks. Although deaf since birth, she had repeatedly asserted that she could avoid danger more easily than hearing people because she was much more sensitive to vibrations, especially from approaching trains, and very loud noises, such as those from blaring train whistles. She was wrong.

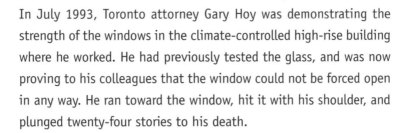

In July 1993, Toronto attorney Gary Hoy was demonstrating the strength of the windows in the climate-controlled high-rise building where he worked. He had previously tested the glass, and was now proving to his colleagues that the window could not be forced open in any way. He ran toward the window, hit it with his shoulder, and plunged twenty-four stories to his death.

Bored between long takes on the set of his 1980s television show *Cover Up,* actor Jon-Erik Hexum grabbed a prop pistol he knew was loaded with blanks. He put it to his head and said, "Let's see if it's got one for me." Even without bullets, a gun loaded with blanks discharges with great force. Hexum died when chunks of his own skull blew into his brain.

Todd Hall from Scottown, Ohio, couldn't wait to light his newly purchased Fourth of July firecrackers, so he touched the lit end of his cigarette to the fuses while he was still inside the store. The 1996 blaze killed nine people. Eleven others were injured in the stampede when customers ran screaming out of the store.

In July 1989, five men from the same farming family died after falling into a manure pit. The first man to enter the pit was quickly overcome by toxic gases and lost consciousness. The others followed one at a time, each attempting to save the one who had gone in before him. A carpet installer working at the farmhouse also tried to help, but was pulled out by his assistant. The five men were finally dragged out of the pit by a local farm equipment salesman. He and two of his employees were the only ones to attempt the rescue using the rope that was hanging in the barn near the manure pit.

While vacationing at the Sandy Balls Holiday Centre in southeastern England in 2002, 11-year-old Scott West aimed a toy dart gun at himself, fired, and died. He choked to death when the dart became lodged in his throat.

A 63-year-old German retiree ran a high-voltage cable into his vegetable patch to wipe out the moles in his garden in 2007. The voltage was enough to run a cement mixer. The man electrocuted himself on the first try. The moles survived.

A helicopter carrying a nuclear research scientist, the deputy director of a radiation laboratory, and other luminaries went down in shallow water in California in 1958. The chopper landed on its side, with the main cabin door underwater. Some of the people on board were able to escape through the windows on the exposed side. With the cabin rapidly filling with water, one of the bright minds still inside the helicopter decided to pull the cord that inflated a twenty-man life raft. The raft immediately blocked the few remaining exits. All of the passengers had survived the crash, but the ones trapped inside the chopper drowned.

In the mid-1980s, Vladmir Boronov, a blacksmith from Irkutsk, Russia, found an old artillery shell left over from the war, and used it as an anvil for more than ten years. He was blown to bits one day when his hammer hit the shell in just the right place.

A man by the last name of Arnes was the owner of a McDonald's franchise in Ellensburg, Washington. He was driving west along Interstate 90 in Washington in 2006 when he crashed his truck. His vehicle had crossed the median and the eastbound lanes before hitting a guardrail. Mr. Arnes climbed out of the wreckage, took off his clothes, and stood naked in the middle of the road. In no time at all, he was run over and killed by an oncoming pickup truck.

A saguaro is the giant variety of cactus that grows in the southwestern United States. What distinguishes them from other cacti is that they look like they are holding their "arms" up in the air. Saguaros can live up to 300 years, weigh as much as 8 tons, and easily grow to heights of more than 50 feet.

On an otherwise uneventful day in 1982, David Grundman and his roommate decided to go into the Arizona desert and play with their guns. They came upon some saguaros and, finding them irresistible targets, began shooting them. After having decimated one small saguaro, Grundman next approached a 26-foot-tall specimen, shooting it multiple times in the trunk. The saguaro toppled over and crushed Grundman to death.

In 2001, Caleb Rebh's Halloween job was to jump out of the woods and scare people when they rode by on the back of a hay truck. Certain he could do better, he climbed up a tree and took the place of a hanging skeleton that was rigged to drop down when the caravan passed by. Caleb carefully arranged the ropes to make sure his feet touched the ground so he wouldn't accidentally hang himself. When the caravan approached, he leapt from the tree. The branch whipped back and choked him to death anyway.

Avery Rowland and Michael Talbot, two inmates from the Kentucky State Reformatory, may have missed that episode of *MacGyver* where he's trapped in the back of a garbage truck and the compactor is about to come down and crush him. In July of 2005, the prisoners hid in a dumpster that was to be unloaded into a garbage truck the following morning. Their crushed bodies were found the next day in a nearby landfill.

Barry Ripley thought Seaford Head in East Sussex, England, was the perfect breezy spot to teach a kid to fly a kite on that beautiful day in September 2004. He handed the kite to his girlfriend's son, took hold of the spool of string, and ran ahead of the boy to get some wind under the kite. If he had been looking straight ahead instead of at the kite, he might have been able to avoid falling off the edge of that 150-foot seaside cliff. Ripley died on impact. The boy and the kite were unharmed.

Jennifer Strange died after competing in the radio contest "Hold Your Wee for a Wii" in Rancho Cordova, California in 2007. The radio show promised the Nintendo video-game system to the person who could drink the most water without going to the bathroom. Jennifer died of water intoxication. The radio station fired all ten of the morning show's staff.

Despite the fact that this incident made international headlines, just one week later, another California radio station ran a similar contest. They offered a free pool table to the winner of their own version of the endurance test. The winner, David Gross of Victorville, got his pool table, which is now collecting dust in his basement; he refuses to use it. He also got to spend a day in the hospital and was out of work for two weeks after suffering the often-fatal effects of water intoxication.

A pizza delivery man was beaten to death in September 2000 by four teenage geniuses who decided this was the way to get some free food. They took all of the victim's pizzas, but left the $600 that was in the man's pocket.

In 2002, Chante Mallard, a nurse's aide from Fort Worth, Texas, hit a homeless man with her car, then drove home with him still stuck to her windshield. When she was arrested, she denied that she had ignored the man's cries for help for three days, and let him bleed to death in her garage. However, she did not dispute the fact that her boyfriend had dumped the man's body in a nearby park.

After having a bit too much to drink one night in 2005, a 29-year-old woman from Belgium took a shortcut through a cemetery on her way home from the bar. At some point in the journey, she felt she could no longer "hold it," so she crouched between two graves and relieved herself. One of the headstones toppled over and crushed her to death.

Frustrated and angry over not being able to pay his real estate taxes, a 56-year-old Slovakian man identified only as Frantisek took a homemade guillotine to the local tax office in 2002 and set about the task of chopping off his own head. The device did not decapitate him, but it mangled him so badly that he died anyway.

Tamilselvi, a 37-year-old woman from India, did not believe the doctors when they told her that her two teenage sons' congenital blindness was incurable. The woman killed herself anyway in 2005 so that each son could receive one of her eyes. Now the boys are blind *and* orphaned.

The line that separates the virtual world and the one the rest of us inhabit sometimes becomes a little blurry for certain dedicated on-line gamers. In January 2005, Xiao Yi jumped from the top of a twenty-four-story building in China, believing he would end up in cyberspace with his "real friends," all of whom were characters in his Internet role-playing game.

A surgeon and a university professor from Uzbekistan were also a husband-and-wife team of part-time travel agents. The two were arrested in 2001 on charges that they were killing off customers with the intention of selling their organs to brokers in Russia. Authorities found six bodies, dozens of passports, and about $40,000 in U.S. currency in the couple's home.

At a 2002 gathering of friends one night in Daventry, England, Kevin Barnes fashioned a make-believe pipe bomb from a firecracker. He put the improbable device in his mouth, flicked a lighter, and chuckled, "Tick, tick, boom!" The fuse flickered and fizzled. Then the firecracker exploded. Barnes died of his self-inflicted head injuries.

In 1930s New York, five bar buddies came up with the perfect get-rich-quick scheme: Take out a life insurance policy on a homeless man, kill him, and collect the benefits. Michael Malloy, the lucky bum, was the perfect foil—barely lucid, always drunk, and hardly able to remain upright even on his best days. The Murder Trust, as they would be known, obtained three policies totaling less than $1,800, with a double-indemnity clause if Malloy died accidentally.

One of the members of the Trust owned a bar. The men decided that the least-conspicuous way to kill Malloy was to help him finish drinking himself to death. Malloy came back night after night, no worse for the wear, so the bartender started serving him shots of antifreeze. That had no less an adverse effect on him than whiskey. They tried turpentine, horse liniment, and rat poison. Malloy couldn't tell the difference between any of those either, and continued to show up every night for his free drinks. He even loved the sandwiches made of spoiled sardines, carpet tacks, and tin can shavings he was served with his turpentine one night.

Frustrated and desperate, the gang finally took Malloy to a deserted intersection in the Bronx. After getting him drunk on antifreeze, they ran him over with a car a couple of times. Triumph at last.

Two weeks later, Malloy walked into the bar and apologized for his absence. He had recently had to spend some time in the hospital, he told them.

All out of fresh ideas for disposing of Malloy in any subtle way, the Trust took him upstairs to the bartender's room. They ran a hose from the gas stove to Malloy's mouth and waited for him to turn purple. The next morning, finally, Malloy was dead.

Thinning the Herd

In the end, the Murder Trust was its own nemesis. Suspicious of one another, they began talking to people outside the group. They were eventually caught and stood trial. All five went to prison. Four of them got the electric chair.

A deadly combination of beer, bonfire, and college students claimed the life of Sean Caselli of New Milford, Connecticut, in October 2006. Caselli was standing at what would ordinarily have been a safe distance from the bonfire when someone tossed an empty beer keg into the blaze. The keg exploded, sending shrapnel hurtling through the air. Caselli was nearly decapitated.

Police gave chase to a young man driving erratically on his moped through the quiet streets of Syracuse, Indiana, in April 2005. The 26-year-old, perhaps in fear of being cited for drunk biking, decided to outrun the police cruiser. He revved the bike and pushed it to its limits—a whole 40 miles per hour—and crashed into a tree. He died on impact.

In what is surely the most dangerous and idiotic schoolyard game ever devised by children, 32-year-old Janet Rudd choked to death on a mouthful of marshmallows at the 2006 Western Ontario fair. The winner of the game is the person who can stuff the most marshmallows in his or her mouth without swallowing them, and still be able to say "Chubby Bunny." The losers are usually the people who cut off their own air supply with an unmovable gob of marshmallow, as Janet Rudd did.

In his desire to bring China to greater glory and perhaps become an aeronautical pioneer in the process, a minor officer in the fourteenth century's Ming Dynasty named Wan Hu tried to launch himself into outer space. He tied a rocket to a chair, strapped himself in, and lit the fuse. The contraption exploded, sending him far outward, but not very far upward.

The English explorer John Davis discovered the Falkland Islands off the coast of Antarctica in 1592. The seventy-six-man crew needed to ensure that they would have enough food in their stores to complete the journey home without starving, so they slaughtered 14,000 penguins. As soon as the ship reached the tropics, every bit of the meat spoiled. Of the original seventy-six-man crew, only sixteen returned home alive.

An immigrant teenager in poor health received assistance from the New York City government to be tutored in his home. His teacher, Cheryl Edwards, regularly submitted invoices for her services, and was promptly paid. Government officials became suspicious, however, when they received timesheets totaling 154 hours that she claimed to have worked six months after the boy died in a hospital in Vietnam in January 2006. Edwards insisted that the boy was in New York and not dead while she was tutoring him.

Eri van den Biggelaar had been a teacher for forty years when she was diagnosed with terminal cancer in February 2007. Beloved by faculty and students alike, she was offered a parting gift: The students in shop class built her a casket. While waiting for Ms. van den Biggelaar to die, they kept it in an empty classroom. The younger schoolchildren pretended the coffin was a submarine and used it during playtime.

Ants have been used for centuries in the art and science of Chinese medicine. A Beijing businessman named Wang Zhendong figured out how to make a lucrative business from this bit of knowledge, selling ant farms to practitioners and medical suppliers and promising a 60 percent return on their investment. There were only two small problems: The farms failed to produce any ants, and Wang sold the $25 kits for $1,300 apiece. Wang was sentenced to death in 2007 for swindling $385 million from his customers.

In 1998, Hugo Weicht threw a giant party to mark his twentieth anniversary as a master brewer. In the middle of the celebration, Weicht took a dive into a giant vat of beer. Friends and relatives at the party were unable to pull him out. He drowned in his own brew.

Thinning the Herd

In October 2003, Dragan Radoslavjevic was charged with defrauding the government of more than $68,000 in housing benefits. Distraught and determined not to spend a moment of time in jail, he locked himself in his bathroom and power-drilled a hole into his own head.

The original plan for defeating the Indians at Little Bighorn in 1876 was for the troops under the command of generals Crook, Gibbon, and Custer to surround the tribe's encampment from all sides, and then massacre all the Indians. Custer had a better idea: He and his men would do it all themselves.

By all appearances, they arrived at Little Bighorn first. Custer was ecstatic. He had no idea that Chief Crazy Horse had already disposed of Crook and his men, and that Gibbon and his guys were moseying along at their own slow pace, still far behind. Custer split his men into three groups and ordered them to surround Chief Sitting Bull's sparsely populated encampment.

Thousands of Lakota, Cheyenne, and Arapaho warriors immediately descended upon them. By the time the dust had settled, General George Armstrong Custer and all two hundred of his men were smeared and splattered all along the banks of the Little Bighorn River.

Dominga Atherton and her daughter Gertrude were not very nice people. They frequently humiliated George, Gertrude's husband, in public, referring to him as "the weaker sex." One day in 1887, George received an invitation to visit friends in Chile. He jumped at the chance to escape the torments of his contemptuous wife and mother-in-law. Sadly, poor hapless George suffered kidney failure on board the ship long before reaching Chile. Unsure of what else to do, the captain stored George in a barrel of rum to preserve him, then transferred him, barrel and all, to another ship heading back home to San Francisco.

As luck would have it, the pickled George arrived on Gertrude's doorstep several days before the note the captain had written explaining what had happened. Dominga and Gertrude were soon forced to leave the lavish residence, half crazy and convinced the house was haunted by George's ghost.

In 1925, experienced cave explorer Floyd Collins went looking for a new entrance from Crystal Cave in Kentucky to the nearby Mammoth Cave. A rock fell on him, trapping him inside for more than two weeks. When his body was finally recovered, Floyd was given a decent burial in the family plot. The incident was such a sensation, however, that his family exhumed the body and placed it in a glass casket at the entrance to the cave, making it one of the most ghoulish and lucrative tourist attractions in 1920s America. All went well until someone stole the corpse. The body was later returned, but, strangely, Floyd's left leg was missing. It was never found.

In 1896, two men from Wilder, Kentucky, killed a woman and used her severed head in a satanic Mass. The men were sentenced to hang, but the court was willing to make a deal: Their sentences would be commuted to life in prison if they disclosed the location of the woman's missing head. The men turned down the offer. They were afraid of incurring the wrath of the Devil this late in the game.

A railroad boardinghouse in Waurika, Oklahoma, was the site of a botched burglary attempt in the 1890s. The robber broke into the house at suppertime without stopping to consider the types of people most likely to rent rooms at such a location. Several enormous railroad workers got up from the dinner table and beat the intruder to death. They threw him into an empty car on a northbound train, leaving his corpse to become somebody else's problem. The boardinghouse is now a quaint little tearoom and antiques shop.

Over the years, Mrs. Purcell's patience wore rather thin with regard to her brilliant husband, English composer Henry Purcell. Annoyed that he had not yet arrived from the theater hours after the performance had ended, she locked him out of the house to teach him a lesson. Purcell died of exposure. England buried him in the floor of Westminster Abbey, next to the church's massive pipe organ.

Phyllis Parker, whose father owned the Vealtown Tavern during the American Revolutionary War, fell in love with Dr. Bynam, a tenant at the inn. Shortly after they were married, Bynam was exposed as a British spy and was hanged for treason. General Anthony Wayne had his corpse delivered in a box to the inn. Not knowing what was inside, Phyllis opened the crate and was greeted by the bug-eyed corpse of her husband. She never recovered from the fright.

Thinning the Herd

A group of coworkers in India were engaged in a little harmless horseplay one fine day, as was their habit. As a joke, one of them grabbed an air-pump hose and released a blast of compressed air right between the back pockets of his buddy's pants, inadvertently blowing up his intestines.

Henry David Thoreau, American author and transcendentalist best known for his reflections on living simply and in harmony with nature, contracted tuberculosis in his late teens in 1835. He suffered the effects of this disease on and off for nearly thirty years. His fatal mistake may have been deciding to go outside late one rainy night to count the rings on a tree stump. He developed bronchitis and uttered these final, immortal words: "Moose. Indian."

8

PLAY BALL!

NOBODY IN FOOTBALL SHOULD BE CALLED A GENIUS.
A GENIUS IS A GUY LIKE NORMAN EINSTEIN.

—Joe Theismann

GUTS. PASSION. SKILL. Luck. Strength. Fearlessness. It takes all of these things to achieve a spectacularly stupid death.

It is a mistake, however, to assume that all jocks are dumb and, therefore, more likely than the rest of us to die weirdly. In this respect, their fans can be equally stupid.

Yet, there is something poignant, even poetic, about the death of an athlete or a devoted fan. No matter how they die, with dignity or without it, one thing is certain: Their lives, and those of us who make a sport of observing them, are infinitely richer for their great love of the game.

The ancient Greek athlete Arrichion was a two-time champion of a particularly violent Olympic event called *Pakration*, a wrestling-choking-finger-breaking sort of game. In his third bid for the crown in 564 BC, Arrichion's opponent jumped on his back and tried to strangle him from behind (a perfectly legal move in those days). Arrichion countered the attack by wrenching his upper body with such enormous speed and force that his opponent flew off his back and fell to the ground. The man broke his ankle, and Arrichion broke his own neck. The judges proclaimed Arrichion the winner before realizing the great athlete was dead. They placed the laurel crown on his head anyway.

Hockey player Bill Barilko scored the winning goal that won the Toronto Maple Leafs the Stanley Cup in 1951. A few months later, Barilko was killed in a plane crash while on a fishing trip with friends. His body was found eleven years later.

During the years between Barilko's death and the discovery of his body, the Maple Leafs did not win the Stanley Cup a single time. They won it again the year Barilko's body was found.

A ferryboat hit a well-lit reef in September 2000 and sank off the coast of Paros, Greece. At least ninety persons on board were killed. The crew had put the boat on autopilot so they could watch a soccer match.

A Boston woman in a rowdy crowd celebrating the Red Sox's defeat of the New York Yankees in the 2004 American League Championship Series was killed when a policeman fired a pepper-spray pellet gun. Ordinarily, these pellets are nonlethal, but this one hit Victoria Snelgrove in the eyeball. The cop later said he was actually aiming at some other unruly fan.

Paul Harding's boat ran aground off the coast of Long Island in May 2005. He figured the easiest way out of this predicament was to drop anchor and go belowdecks to wait for high tide to free the boat. While he waited, a jet-skier named John Wilson ran directly through the anchor line and was decapitated.

Thinning the Herd

A boring old coffin in a stuffy funeral parlor just wouldn't do for die-hard Pittsburgh Steelers fan James Smith. When he died in 2005, Smith's friends and family brought his easy chair to the Coston Funeral Home and asked the mortician to prop him up in it. They dressed him in his gold and black pajamas, robe, and slippers, put the remote control in his hand, and placed a pack of cigarettes and a beer on a small table nearby. Throughout the wake, a high-definition television set played Steelers highlights on a continuous loop.

Mexican female wrestler Juana Barraza, known professionally as "The Silent One," shared a house with her mother. Despite these living arrangements, the two women had not spoken to each other in many years. Rather than allow the silence and strife to embitter her personal life, Barraza successfully channeled her rage into her on-stage persona.

Barraza was arrested in Mexico City in 2006 and identified as the vicious serial killer *Mataviejitas* (Killer of Little Old Ladies). She was accused of strangling as many as thirty elderly women. Barraza later told police that the victims reminded her of her mother.

Fortunately for the 84,000 people inside the University of Oklahoma's football stadium in October 2005, a would-be suicide bomber succeeded only in blowing himself up. Few people in the crowd even noticed the disturbance, which occurred about 100 yards from the stadium. One witness said she saw a little smoke, but no more than would have risen from a small barbecue grill at any one of the numerous tailgate parties in the parking lot.

Former French rugby captain Marc Cecillon sought solace in a bottle after his retirement from professional sports. While attending a large party in 2004, he slapped a woman in the face. The hosts asked Cecillon to leave. When Cecillon's wife refused to go with him, he left her there. He returned to the party a short time later with his revolver and shot her. In court, Cecillon testified that this was all a misunderstanding. He had only meant to convince his wife that he was serious about them leaving the party together.

A New Jersey woman's head was found inside her own bowling bag in March 2005. Authorities found a few more of her body parts hidden behind the walls of her house. A man who had lived with the woman for a while was strongly suspected of knowing something about this.

For centuries, many Middle Eastern countries have welcomed the arrival of spring with elaborately staged kite festivals. In each village, virtually every inhabitant participates in the colorful ritual. Skillful kite fliers prepare spools of string covered with shards of glass, razors, and wire, and engage in a sort of duel. The idea is to crisscross kite strings until the opponents' kites are cut loose and sent billowing into the stratosphere or plummeting back to earth.

In 2005, Pakistan banned the annual festival after nineteen people were killed. One man was decapitated by a razor-sharp kite string, and over two hundred others were injured.

Despite the fact that Thailand has never competed in a soccer World Cup match, two very enthusiastic Thai men cheered loudly for the Italian team while watching the 2006 games on a television in a restaurant in Bangkok. One of the restaurant patrons, unappreciative of the noise, asked the men to please quiet down. When they refused, the diner shot them both at point-blank range.

Rather than walk to retrieve a stray golf ball near the fifth hole of the Palos Verdes Golf Club, 50-year-old Mickey Ganiel of California drove his cart off the service road and up the hill. On the way down, he lost control of the vehicle, flipped over, and was crushed to death by the cart.

Devan Young, a 29-year-old night maintenance worker from Wichita, Kansas, was found dead by his coworkers early one morning in 2003. He was trapped in the pin-resetting machine in the bowling alley where he worked the night shift.

Legendary hothead Len Koenecke was cut from the Dodgers baseball team for disciplinary reasons in 1935. On board a chartered flight the following day, Koenecke got drunk and started a fight with the crew, demanding to take control of the plane. The crew used a fire extinguisher to put an end to the altercation. They hit Koenecke over the head with it, bludgeoning him to death.

Thinning the Herd

Albert Short was an English hot-air balloon enthusiast and aircraft designer in the 1920s and 1930s. After safely landing one of his seaplanes, he dropped dead of a heart attack right in his own cockpit.

In 1953, jockey Frank Hayes suffered a heart attack during a horse race. The horse, Sweet Kiss, went on to finish first, making Hayes the only dead jockey ever to win a race.

Vladimir Smirnov, a champion fencer from the Soviet Union, suffered a fatal injury before a live audience during the 1982 Olympics. His opponent's foil pierced Smirnov's mask, entered his eyeball, and lanced his brain. Smirnov died nine days later.

In 1983, professional diver Sergei Chalibashvili attempted the Dive of Death—a three-and-a-half reverse somersault in the tuck position. He jumped up, hit the board with his head, tumbled through the air several times, crashed into the water, and sank to the bottom of the pool. He was most likely dead long before he hit the water.

In November 2006, gymnastics instructor John McCurdy III performed a near-perfect quadruple front flip from a trampoline at his gym in North Carolina. The trampoline was surrounded by protective foam padding 6 feet deep. McCurdy "stuck the landing"—with his head. He had successfully completed three of the four flips when his head slipped neatly between the foam cubes and hit the concrete slab underneath.

Jonathan Figueroa, whose family had moved from Brooklyn, New York, to Allentown, Pennsylvania, returned to his old neighborhood as often as he could. He missed his familiar surroundings, his girlfriend, and his favorite sport: elevator surfing (riding on the tops of elevators in motion). He was found dead at the bottom of an elevator shaft with a crushed skull in December 2006.

Thinning the Herd

In the summer of 2003, Stephen Hilder, a 20-year-old veteran sky-diver, cut the straps of his parachute rig with a pair of scissors and plunged 13,000 feet to his death in Wiltshire, England, for no apparent reason. Friends and witnesses reported that Hilder appeared "jubilant" and "excited" on the way down. Hilder had recently broken up with his girlfriend and converted to Catholicism.

Danish cyclist Knut Jensen died during the 1960 Rome Olympics. He collapsed of sunstroke in the middle of the race. Blood tests later revealed the presence of amphetamines and a metabolism booster. He might have survived either one of these conditions but he seriously injured himself when he landed on his head.

A 19-year-old man named Jeff Bailey died of a heart attack after scoring 16,660 on Berzerk, a popular video arcade game of the early 1980s. This was the first known instance of dying—for real—while playing a video game.

Douglas Mitchell, a 58-year-old top-ranked archer from England, was killed with his own bow in 2002. Mitchell was handling the bow in his workshop when part of the assembly broke apart and struck Mitchell in the head.

Heli-skiing is the sport in which thrill-seekers are dropped from a helicopter onto very high cliffs. They then ski to the bottom in an almost vertical descent. Approximately forty heli-skiers have been killed since the sport became popular in the 1970s.

In 1994, helicopter pilot Dave Walton took Walt Disney president Frank Wells, documentary filmmaker Beverly Johnson, and their friend Paul Scannell to the remote Ruby Mountains of Nevada. The helicopter crashed just before the heli-skiers jumped out. All four were killed.

South Korean boxer Duk Koo Kim was killed in the ring in 1982 after going fourteen rounds with Ray "Boom Boom" Mancini. To minimize the risk of this ever happening again, the World Boxing Association shortened the maximum number of rounds from fifteen to twelve.

Thinning the Herd

Cleveland Indians teammates Bob Ojeda, Steve Olin, and Tim Crews took a break from Spring Training just before the start of the 1993 baseball season. They went fishing off the coast of Florida and slammed their boat into a pier. Olin and Crews died in the accident. Ojeda survived, but had to have his scalp surgically reattached.

In 1978, Angels outfielder Lyman Bostock was traveling by car with his uncle and two female companions in Gary, Indiana. A man in another car pulled up alongside them and fired a gun. The bullet killed Bostock. The shooter turned out to be the estranged husband of one of the women, who was his intended target.

Second-string catcher for the Cincinnati Reds, Willard Hershberger, became distraught after the pitch he called turned into a game-winning grand-slam home run for the Boston Braves during the 1940 World Series. After the game, Hershberger went to his hotel room, meticulously laid towels on the bathroom floor, knelt before the bathtub, and slit his throat open with his roommate's razor.

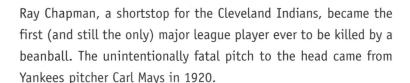

Ray Chapman, a shortstop for the Cleveland Indians, became the first (and still the only) major league player ever to be killed by a beanball. The unintentionally fatal pitch to the head came from Yankees pitcher Carl Mays in 1920.

Mike "Doc" Powers was a catcher in the first game ever played in Shibe Park in Philadelphia in 1909. He crashed into a wall going after a pop fly, hitting it hard enough to give himself internal injuries. He finished the game, but died two weeks later.

Problematic baseball player Ed Delahanty was suspended in 1903 by the Washington Nationals for a number of violations. He decided to take a trip to get away from the conflict, and boarded a train to Niagara Falls. Ordered off the train for drunk and disorderly conduct, he fell through a drawbridge and into Niagara Falls.

In 1964, Mark Maples became the first person to be killed in Disneyland. As the Matterhorn bobsled he was riding reached the top of the mountain, Mark undid his seat belt and stood up. He was promptly hurled onto the tracks below.

While competing in the 1958 Tour of Gippsland in Melbourne, Australia, cyclist and two-time Olympic medalist Russell Mockridge died just 2 miles from the start of the race. He had been hit by an oncoming bus.

On the evening before the 1996 Super Bowl game in New Orleans, professional bungee jumper Laura Patterson was rehearsing what was to have been the grand finale of the twelve-minute halftime show. Patterson jumped from the top of a specially built tower inside the stadium and landed on her head. She was killed instantly. The volunteers had let out too much of the bungee cord.

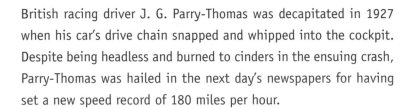

British racing driver J. G. Parry-Thomas was decapitated in 1927 when his car's drive chain snapped and whipped into the cockpit. Despite being headless and burned to cinders in the ensuing crash, Parry-Thomas was hailed in the next day's newspapers for having set a new speed record of 180 miles per hour.

"Ghost riding the whip" is a relatively new automotive sport that is rapidly gaining popularity, particularly among West Coast fans of hip-hop music. "Ghost riding" refers to traveling in a car with no driver; "whip" is urban slang for automobile. Ghost riders typically put the car in neutral, get out, and begin dancing around or on top of the slow-moving vehicle. Sometimes they just let go of the wheel and stick their bodies out of the car.

Davender Gulley of Stockton, California, was very good at ghost riding, until his head slammed into a parked car while he was hanging out of the window of his SUV.

Former track star Andrew Rhoades of Massachusetts was affable and full of confidence all his short life. During Thanksgiving week-end in 2006, he came upon an opportunity he couldn't resist. He decided to drop in on some friends staying in the apartment building next door by jumping from the roof of his building to their roof across the alley. He assessed the 20-foot gap between the two buildings and figured it was an easy enough jump. His wristwatch was the only part of him that actually landed on the neighboring rooftop. A few scratch marks were found on the rubber edge of the ledge. His mangled body was discovered several hours later in the alley.

At the 1977 South African Grand Prix, track marshal Jansen Van Vuuren ran across the track with a fire extinguisher to attend to a race car that had caught fire. Before he got to the other side of the track, he was hit by the Formula One car being driven by Tom Pryce. Van Vuuren died on impact. Pryce, who had survived the fire, was killed when the fire extinguisher flew out of Van Vuuren's hands and hit Pryce in the face.

Bob Moose, a pitcher for the Pittsburgh Pirates, died in a car accident in 1976. He was on his way to his own birthday party.

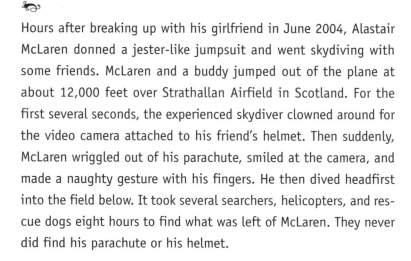

Hours after breaking up with his girlfriend in June 2004, Alastair McLaren donned a jester-like jumpsuit and went skydiving with some friends. McLaren and a buddy jumped out of the plane at about 12,000 feet over Strathallan Airfield in Scotland. For the first several seconds, the experienced skydiver clowned around for the video camera attached to his friend's helmet. Then suddenly, McLaren wriggled out of his parachute, smiled at the camera, and made a naughty gesture with his fingers. He then dived headfirst into the field below. It took several searchers, helicopters, and rescue dogs eight hours to find what was left of McLaren. They never did find his parachute or his helmet.

An online virtual reality game enthusiast named Qiu Chengwei was sentenced to death in Shanghai in 2005 for fatally stabbing his friend. The two had argued over the rightful ownership of an imaginary sword.

At a horse race in Loreto, Mexico, in 2006, the two front-runners were approaching the finish line neck-and-neck. A young man named José Bernardo González suddenly jumped from the stands and stood in the path of the oncoming horses. From what friends and witnesses could later gather, it appeared that González wanted to make sure that the horse he had bet on would win. The only sure thing that day was González's skull getting crushed in the stampede.

Neil Roberts of Britain took a trip to Las Vegas and sent loads of happy notes and letters back home, regaling loved ones with the tales of his American adventure. "Got a win . . . $1,100 on roulette," read one e-mail. "Seen Elton John. Was quite good," he wrote to a friend. In a postcard to his mother, he talked about how exhausting gambling could be, but told her not to worry. "I am sensible so I won't blow my savings." He told her of his plans to see the Grand Canyon by helicopter, and maybe buy a ticket to a magic show. On February 9, 2006, Roberts threw himself off the top of the 100-story Stratosphere Casino.

Workers at a lumberyard near San Francisco's Golden Gate Bridge established a unique sort of club in the 1980s—the Golden Gate

Leapers Association. They take bets on which day of the week someone will jump. At least one person takes the plunge every couple of weeks.

Barney Doyle of Fairfield, New Jersey, took it easy after heart problems forced him to retire from his railroad job, but he never missed a Giants game. One beautiful Sunday afternoon in 1950, he and a buddy headed across the river to the old Polo Grounds stadium in the Bronx for a doubleheader between the Giants and the Dodgers. As they sat in their upper-tier bandstand seats at the start of the first game, Doyle was hit in the head by a bullet and was killed instantly. As paramedics carried Doyle's bloodied body out of the park, fans fought over his seat.

Police later found 14-year-old Robert Peebles, who confessed to shooting a .45-caliber automatic pistol into the air from the roof of his apartment building, not far from the stadium. Because of his age, Peebles was only charged with juvenile delinquency. It would have pleased Barney Doyle to know that the Giants beat the Dodgers 5 to 4 in the first game.

Thinning the Herd

Long Beach State football coach George Allen Sr. was as obsessed with winning as he was with pushing himself and his college team to their absolute limits. His players loved him anyway. After winning the last game of a particularly tough season, the team dumped the traditional tub of ice water over the head of their 68-year-old coach. It gave him pneumonia.

In the coming days, Allen would refuse his doctor's advice to take it easy until he recovered, and scoffed at the idea of a pacemaker for his irregular heartbeat. He went out for a vigorous run on New Year's Eve 1990, as he did every afternoon. His wife later found him on the floor of their den, dead of a massive heart attack.

In 1996, David Bailey of Clondalkin, Ireland, went to retrieve a golf ball from a ditch near the first hole. His sudden approach frightened a rat, which ran up his pant leg and peed on him. His friends urged Bailey to go back to the clubhouse and shower, but he assured them it was no big deal. He wiped the urine off and seeing no bites or scratches, continued with the game. A week later, Bailey was dead of kidney failure brought on by a case of the rare but deadly Weil's disease.

Tom and Eileen Lonergan of Louisiana were on a scuba-diving expedition in 1998 in the shark-infested waters off Australia's Great Barrier Reef. The boat that had taken their group of divers out to sea inadvertently left the Lonergans behind. The two were never seen again.

The World Wrestling Federation had arranged for Owen Hart to win a match in 1999. In typically splashy style, Hart was lowered into the ring from the stadium rafters, clad brilliantly in his Blue Blazer costume, replete with cape and feathers. With less than 80 feet to go, the cable snapped loose. Owen entered the ring with a splat in front of 16,000 fans. The ecstatic crowd roared, thinking it was part of the show. After several minutes, the master of ceremonies announced, "Folks, we've got a problem here."

Otto Lilienthal was a German pioneer in the earliest days of aviation. Wilbur and Orville Wright used many of Lilienthal's calculations on lift and aerodynamics in the early 1900s, despite some errors that sent the Wright brothers back to the drawing board on numerous occasions. In 1896, while experimenting with a hang glider he had just designed, Lilienthal crashed into a field. He died of his injuries two days later.

Georgi Markov was a Bulgarian dissident and Olympic weight-lifting gold medalist. In 1978, an unidentified man with an accent stepped out of a London crowd and shot Markov in the leg with a specially rigged umbrella. The pellet that embedded itself in Markov's calf was full of ricin poison. The assassin got away in a taxi.

An empty inflatable kayak washed up early one morning in 2007 on a beach in Kaikoura, New Zealand. There was some fishing gear on board, an empty potato chip bag, and a half-drunk soda bottle on the floor, but no other sign of the kayak's owner. An astute police sergeant told the press, "Indications are that a person should have been with it."

One of the strangest spectator sports in all of history has to be jumper-gawking at the Mihara-Yama volcano in Japan. It began as a twisted sort of spiritual journey in 1933, when 24-year-old Mieko Ueki painted a lovely image in words for her friend, Masako Tomita. Standing at the lip of the volcano, Mieko told Masako that jumping into the bubbling lava would be a beautiful way to die—instantly cremated and then rising to heaven in a billowing swirl of smoke. Masako protested a bit, but then agreed not to interfere. The two young women bowed respectfully to one another. Masako stepped aside, and Mieko jumped in.

News of the "poetic suicide" spread quickly, and inspired nearly a thousand others to leap into the stinking lava. Many thousands more came to watch. Steamship service to the volcano doubled. Roadside stands, tourist stops, hotels, and restaurants popped up all over the place. The Japanese government eventually limited access to the area, but not until the economy had been given a fair chance to benefit from this unexpected boon.

It took thirty-five years for divers to recover the remains of Donald Campbell and his Bluebird boat from the bottom of Coniston Water, a lake in northwestern England. Campbell had been trying to break his own speed record in 1967. As he approached his previous top speed of 276 miles per hour, the boat gracefully rose out of the water, did a few quadruple backflips, and then sank nose-first, 150 feet below the surface of the lake. Campbell remained in radio contact while his boat completed its gymnastics routine. "The water's dark green and I can't see a bloody thing! Hallo, the bow is up! I'm going. I'm on my back! I'm gone."

CHAPTER

9

BETTER LUCK
NEXT TIME

EVERYBODY KNOWS THAT THE GREAT RUSSIAN POET MAIAKOVSKY
COMMITTED SUICIDE. WHAT IS NOT SO WELL KNOWN IS THAT
HIS LAST WORDS WERE, "COMRADES, DON'T SHOOT."
—Fred Botten

THERE HAVE BEEN times, while doing the dishes, for example, that a glass has slipped through my soapy fingers, dropped into the sink, ricocheted off a dish, bounced onto the counter, then plunged to the floor, only to survive the harrowing experience with nary a scratch. Another glass from the same set may shatter into a million pieces if I so much as drop an ice cube into it the wrong way.

People can be equally fragile, and just as mind-bogglingly resilient. Against all odds, and no matter how right it would otherwise be, some of them just won't die.

In 2005, a 21-year-old man from Murdoch, Australia, created a beer-drinking device that consisted of a helmet connected to a keg via a hose, and powered by an electric drill. The contraption, he hoped, would allow him to consume large quantities of beer in record time. The force with which the beer shot out of the keg ripped open the man's stomach. Amazingly, he lived.

Karl Barton-Harvey, a drunk and depressed man living in Wiltshire, England, set fire to his apartment in a botched suicide attempt after an argument with his wife. "Once his hair caught fire," a judge explained in the court's decision to let stand Karl's 2001 arson conviction, "he decided it wasn't such a good idea, and jumped out of the window to safety."

In 2004, a man registered as a guest at The Inn at Bingham School in Mebane, North Carolina, was hoping to die quietly in a beautiful, peaceful place. Once in his room, he disconnected the propane gas line attached to the fireplace and lay himself down on the soft, comfortable bed. He blew up the historic home, and suffered only minor burns in the explosion.

Porn star Mary Carey was forced to drop out of the 2003 California governor's race against Arnold Schwarzenegger when her mother jumped off the roof of a four-story building in Florida. The mother survived. Mary's political career did not.

Distraught over the belief that his wife was having an affair, Alfonse Mumbo of Kenya cut off his own penis and testicles with a kitchen knife in 2003. Unfortunately for him, he lived. Mrs. Mumbo denied ever having an affair.

In 2007, an Atlanta apartment manager was handed a letter by two of her tenants. She soon realized that the letter was a suicide note and immediately contacted the police. The tenants, two men in their early forties, were distraught over the failure of their business.

The officers arrived to find the apartment soaked in blood, a circular saw buzzing, and three of the men's four arms on the floor. Police turned off the saw before the second man could cut off his other arm. Both men survived.

Barbara Graham was a featured speaker at the Million Mom March in Washington, D.C., in the year 2000. She had lost her son to violence and became an outspoken advocate for stricter gun control laws across the nation. A year after her appearance at the march, Graham shot the man she thought was her son's killer. The man lived, but was left paralyzed. Police confirmed that he was not the person who killed Graham's son. Graham was convicted of attempted murder.

Christina Mack of Peoria, Illinois, greased the floor of her kitchen in an attempt to kill her one-legged boyfriend in 1997. She slipped on the floor and knocked herself unconscious instead. Police found more grease near the top of the stairs and by the bathroom door. The boyfriend, Chester Parkman Sr., insisted that Christina was just doing a little housework.

It was Shantie Marjal's job to raise the flag every day in the parking lot of a Pasadena, California, shopping center. When she untied the rope on the flagpole one day in 2006, a shopping cart fell on her head, breaking her neck. A group of pranksters had hoisted the cart to the top of the flagpole as a joke. Shantie survived, but will never be quite the same.

When Christopher Ariola's father asked him to turn off the two radios and the television set he was listening to simultaneously, Christopher beat him over the head with a baseball bat. Racked with guilt over the terrible thing he had done, Christopher decided to kill himself. First he went bowling. Then he slashed his wrists. When that didn't work, he got into his father's Jeep and deliberately crashed it, causing himself minor injuries. He was charged with murder in 2002.

Louise Egan Brunstad, a lovesick and suicidal 16-year-old girl from Atlanta, Georgia, crashed her car into an oncoming vehicle in 2006.

Thinning the Herd

She counted down the seconds before impact in text messages she sent to the female classmate who spurned her. The girl survived. The unfortunate driver of the other car did not.

A 47-year-old Munich man tried to end it all by jumping in front of a train. He missed. He smashed instead through the window of the engine car, seriously frightening the train conductor. The trauma caused the conductor to miss several weeks of work. The courts ordered the man to pay for repairs to the train, and for the conductor's lost wages.

A Tallahassee, Florida, man shot a ring necked duck in 2007 and stored it in a freezer for later consumption. Two days later, the man's wife opened the freezer and was scared nearly to death when the duck placidly lifted its head and looked at her. The duck, now known as Perky, was transported to Goose Creek Wildlife Sanctuary, where she was treated for wounds to her wing and leg. During surgery, however, Perky suffered cardiac arrest. She was successfully resuscitated, thereby cheating death yet again.

In the state of Florida, teachers are required to take certification exams every five years in order to keep their teaching licenses. After learning that she had failed the test in 2006, Patti Withers decided life wasn't worth living. She set out to end it all in the place she loved most: the school where she taught.

Thankfully, Ms. Withers had sense enough to wait until the children were gone before she began popping prescription pills in her empty classroom. She ran out of water before she ran out of pills, so she drove her motorized scooter down the hallway to the drinking fountain. Two other teachers became suspicious of her erratic driving and called 911.

Ms. Withers survived her moment of despair and decided to go on with her life after all. The superintendent of schools, however, proposed that Withers be fired on the grounds that attempted suicide was immoral. Withers sued to keep her job. The fact that she had failed the certification exam in the first place was, apparently, insufficient cause for dismissal.

A man from New South Wales, Australia, convinced himself that he was dying of a communicable disease and that he had already infected his wife and children. To spare himself and his family this terrible fate, he decided they should all die. In the middle of his homemade crime spree, he called the police to notify them of the murder-suicide in progress. While waiting for the cops to arrive, he stabbed himself repeatedly, but found that he wasn't dying quickly enough. So he hit himself over the head with a hammer a few times. Police arrived to find the man hiding in a garden shed, severely battered, but still alive.

A 37-year-old Dutch man suffering from hypothermia was hospitalized in The Hague in 2001 after he jumped from a bridge—three times. Police found him leaning over the railing of the bridge, shivering and frostbitten, and about to plunge into the icy waters for the fourth time. Despite the man's obvious determination, it is unclear why he didn't try a different method after the first attempt failed.

In 2006, Amy Dallamura from Aberystwyth, Wales, was banned from her favorite beach resort, its promenade, and the surrounding area after being rescued several times from drowning. One emergency rescue technician almost lost his own life trying to save her when he had to let go of his safety line to swim out an additional 300 meters. Ms. Dallamura was terribly upset over the banishment. She said she never asked to be rescued. She was merely seeking to end her back pain.

Michael Mankamyer got drunk one night in 2007 and jumped off the balcony of his room on board the *Carnival Glory* cruise ship. The crew alerted the Coast Guard and immediately initiated a search. They found Michael about eight hours later, waving frantically from the water. The 35-year-old man suffered mild hypothermia, but was otherwise okay. It probably helped that Michael weighed 300 pounds, which enabled him to float more easily than a skinny person would have been able to until help arrived.

During a 2003 Ku Klux Klan initiation ritual in Tennessee, Gregory Freeman fired several shots into the air. Perhaps not fully grasping the concept of gravity, he never considered that what goes up must come down. The descending bullet struck fellow Klansman Jeff Murr in the head, wounding him critically.

Eric "Black Hole" Storm and his buddy Michael Lewis called New York City police at 2:00 A.M. one night in 2007 and informed them that they and twenty other members of their suicide cult were planning to drink poisoned juice on the steps of City Hall. Snipers and other law enforcement officers immediately descended on the scene, but found no one other than the two 21-year-old men. "Black Hole" and Lewis were transported to Bellevue Hospital's psychiatric ward without further incident.

Alofa Time was distraught after decapitating his wife in 2006. Driving erratically into downtown Boise, Idaho, he attracted the attention of a police cruiser. Time crashed his truck into an oncoming vehicle, killing two more people. On impact, Theresa Time's head flew out of the truck and landed several feet away. Mr. Time got out of the truck and begged police to shoot him. The police let him live. The rest of Mrs. Time was later found in the garage of the couple's home.

A Romanian doctor was treated for severe shock when he was attacked in the morgue by what he thought was a corpse. Bogdan Georgescu, 16, had collapsed while drinking coffee with his brother and was taken to Brasov County Hospital, where he was declared dead on arrival. Some time later, the teenager opened his eyes and found himself surrounded by dead people. When he saw a man in a white coat approaching, he panicked and began swinging. The doctor was given a few days off to recover from the scare and the beating.

Convicted murderer Ruben Dario Ovejero of Tucuman, Argentina, was released from prison in 2005 when the man he was accused of killing strolled back into town one fine April day, drunk but still alive. Pedro Roldan told police that he had no idea people thought he was dead.

Richard Smith was the captain of the Staten Island Ferry that plowed into a New York City pier at full speed in October 2003.

Immediately after the incident, Captain Smith ran home and tried to kill himself. He slashed his wrists, then got a BB gun and shot himself once in the head and once in the heart. He survived. Eleven passengers on his ferry did not.

The family of Julia Warnes received a letter from her utilities company in 2006, advising them to make arrangements to have billing and water services discontinued now that she was dead. Julia had suffered complications during surgery some weeks prior. She herself called the company and told them that she would still need water, especially considering that she was still alive.

A woman from Nuremberg, Germany, called the police one night, alarmed when her boyfriend became suddenly silent while she was talking to him on the phone. Emergency services dispatched a police car, firefighters, and an ambulance to the man's house. The blaring sirens brought the man to the door, where he told officers that he had dozed off during a lull in the conversation.

Master prankster Alan Abel loved staging elaborate hoaxes. Despite having been exposed as a fraud several times over a period of forty years, he was remarkably successful in making otherwise successful and respected people look like dopes. In 1979, he faked his own death to get *The New York Times* to write his obituary. They did. The following day, Abel held a press conference in which he borrowed a line from Mark Twain: "Reports of my demise have been grossly exaggerated."

The British magazine *Melody Maker* took an unusual approach in reviewing an Alice Cooper concert in the 1970s. The critic wrote the review in the form of an obituary. The undisputed king of "shock rock," whose gory onstage shenanigans and signature horror-movie makeup won him millions of fans worldwide, later issued the following statement: "I'm alive, and drunk as usual."

Frank Gorshin, who would go on to earn a place in the annals of classic television history for his role as "The Riddler" on the campy 1960s show *Batman,* fractured his skull in a car accident in 1957.

A Los Angeles newspaper mistakenly reported that he had died in the crash. He was only unconscious for four days.

When a magazine prematurely published Rudyard Kipling's obituary in the 1930s, he wrote them a short note: "I've just read that I am dead. Don't forget to delete me from your list of subscribers."

Benjamin Franklin had a long-standing yet friendly feud with Titan Leeds, who published an almanac that competed with Franklin's *Poor Richard's Almanac*. Franklin made predictions of the date of Leeds's demise in 1733, 1734, 1735, and 1740. Each time the date came and went with Leeds still alive, Franklin published his obituary in his newspaper anyway. Leeds responded every time by writing Franklin letters "from the great beyond."

Dave Swarbrick, a British folk music fiddler, read his own obituary in a 1999 edition of *The Daily Telegraph* of London. Swarbrick took the news with characteristic good humor. "It's not the first time I have died in Coventry," he said.

Abe Vigoda, the elderly, tall, slouching actor known to fans of the 1970s show *Barney Miller* and who played "Sal Tessio" in the movie *The Godfather,* is periodically reported dead by a number of U.S. publications. His current state (dead or alive) is continuously up-dated on his Internet website, www.abevigoda.com.

James McNeill Whistler, creator of the famous 1871 painting known commonly as *Whistler's Mother*, was reported dead in a Dutch news-paper after he suffered a heart attack. Whistler graciously thanked the Dutch newspaper in a note saying, "Reading my own obituary induced a tender glow of health."

About twenty people each year visit the beautiful white chalk cliffs of Beachy Head in England, and jump to their deaths. A few oth-ers are thrown. In July of 2002, one young man took a leap and landed on a ledge about halfway down. He called the Coast Guard on his cell phone and asked them to pick him up; he had changed his mind.

Gary Davies's dog burst into flames when it peed on a live wire. Davies later told the press, "There was an almighty explosion, and the whole street lit up. I turned round, and the dog was on fire." Power was off for five hours that day in Middlestone Moor, England. Against all odds, the dog survived.

CHAPTER

10

WHEN THE
FUR FLIES

EVERY YEAR, at the start of deer hunting season, the editor of a local newspaper in Upstate New York, sets up a tally board in his office: Deer versus People.

I'm not sure if the season has ever ended with more dead people than deer, but I find the idea of someone keeping such a scorecard rather amusing, and oddly comforting. I'm rooting for the deer, of course, and I suspect that editor is, as well.

Now, if it were giant-flying-cockroach hunting season, I might not be so glib.

Dozens of angry fishermen gathered regularly to exact their revenge on Kuno, a 77-pound catfish that leapt out of the water and killed a dachshund in 2001. The pet wiener dog had made the terrible mistake one day of going for a swim in Kuno's lake. Kuno ate him.

For more than two years, Kuno managed to evade capture. However, he was no match for Mother Nature. A drought turned Kuno's pond into not much more than a muddy bog. The fishermen were at last able to trudge right up to the 5-foot-long dog-eater and pluck him out of the shallow waters. Kuno was stuffed and mounted, and now resides above the mantle in a nearby lodge in Mönchengladbach, Germany.

In a show of incomprehensible extravagance, the Roman poet Virgil arranged a funeral for his pet housefly. Virgil spent the modern equivalent of $800,000 on the ceremony, a catered affair that was held in his mansion, replete with orchestra and paid mourners.

A sparrow flew through an open window at a Dutch convention center in 2005 and knocked over 23,000 dominoes. An angry mob cornered the poor, frightened bird, and someone shot it. The senseless killing sparked the outrage of millions around the world. In response, Dutch authorities announced that the sparrow would be preserved as a national treasure. The bird can now be seen at Rotterdam's Natural History Museum, perched on top of a box of dominoes.

In August 2005, a German man was killed by the fish he was trying to catch. The fish latched onto the fishing pole and fought ferociously for control of it. The man lost his balance, fell into the water, and drowned. Police described the fish as "ordinary."

Topsy was a 3-ton elephant whose great size and strength helped build many of the attractions at Coney Island's Luna Park in the late 1800s. Over time, however, Topsy developed a bad temper, the direct result of years of abuse and mishandling. She killed three men in three years.

Thompson and Dundy, who owned Luna Park, decided to make an example—not to mention a quick profit—at Topsy's expense. Shortly after the death of the last sadistic handler in 1903, they announced that Topsy was a menace to mankind and would be publicly hanged.

The ASPCA stepped in immediately, condemning the action. They pointed out that New York State had recently determined that death by hanging constituted cruel and unusual punishment, and had replaced the gallows with its first electric chair. So Thompson and Dundy asked Thomas Edison to arrange the execution. Edison, who had been experimenting on farm animals in his attempts to devise a more efficient electric chair, jumped at the chance to zap an elephant.

Sadly, Topsy was killed for the entertainment and profit of pitiless men. The only mercy was the fact that she died quickly. As fate would have it, however, Topsy got her revenge from beyond the grave. What was left of Luna Park was utterly destroyed in a massive fire of unknown origin in 1931. A memorial to Topsy now stands at the site where she died.

A customs officer stopped Wayne Floyd as he was about to board a flight from Sydney, Australia, to Bangkok, Thailand. There was something suspicious about the weird bulge in Floyd's crotch. A strip search revealed that he was attempting to smuggle six eggs from an endangered species in his underwear. Two of the creatures died in Floyd's makeshift nest. Floyd was sentenced in 2006.

Bruno the Bear went on a seven-week homicidal rampage through Germany and Austria in the summer of 2006. The bear belonged to a northern Italian agency that was working to reintroduce wildlife into the Alps. Bruno was responsible for the deaths of no fewer than twenty-five sheep, four goats, and untold numbers of chickens and rabbits. He stole honey from beehives and squashed a farmer's guinea pig. Authorities finally closed in on the bear and killed him, and later blamed the senseless killings on sexual frustration. Italian authorities immediately demanded that Germany return Bruno to his rightful homeland.

Members of a British cricket club were burning yard debris when a flaming rabbit suddenly shot out from the bonfire and ran into an equipment hut. Fully engulfed, the rabbit set the hut ablaze and caused over $100,000 in damage.

Maurice John McCredden of Manjimup, Australia, was killed in 2006 when an airborne kangaroo crashed through the windshield of his

Thinning the Herd

car. It was not clear whether the kangaroo died in the crash, or if it was already dead when it hit McCredden's car.

In July 2001, a security guard working at a resort in Johannesburg, South Africa, spotted a hippopotamus eating grass on the golf course. He notified his boss immediately. The guard was told to watch the hippo until wildlife officials could be called in to handle the situation. The hippo didn't much care for the way the guard was staring at him, so it charged. The guard was dead by the time the animal experts arrived. They shot the hippo with a tranquilizer dart to subdue it, but the sedative killed the hippo. They later explained that the hippo was probably suffering from high levels of stress.

U.S. Vice President Dick Cheney single-handedly killed more than seventy farm-raised ring-necked pheasants during a 2003 hunting expedition. Along with nine other companions, the men killed a total of 417 pheasants and an undisclosed number of mallard ducks. The birds had been cleverly placed in the controlled environment of a "canned hunt" to make the experience a little less taxing for the vice president and his guests.

Perhaps not wanting to reignite the outrage of impassioned animal advocates, Cheney participated in another hunting expedition three years later, this time in the wide-open spaces of a sprawling Texas ranch. The vice president mistook one of his hunting buddies for a quail, and nearly killed 78-year-old lawyer Harry Whittington of Austin, Texas. Despite the embedded bits of buckshot in his face and torso and the heart attack that followed, Whittington survived.

In its efforts to eradicate malaria in Malaysia in the 1950s, the World Health Organization orchestrated what was perhaps the largest-ever massacre of animals and insects resulting from a single act. After careful study and consideration, they ordered the spraying of DDT over a vast region of the country. This killed off a significant portion of the malaria-carrying mosquitoes, but created a few other problems. First, people's houses began to fall down on top of their heads; it turned out that, along with the mosquitoes, the DDT had also killed the wasps, which allowed their favorite food source—thatch-eating caterpillars—to thrive. Hundreds of thousands of geckos then arrived to devour the billions of dead mosquitoes and wasps. Residual DDT from the insects didn't kill the geckos, but it did give them a severe neurological disorder. In came the cats to feast on the slow-moving geckos. Unfortunately,

Thinning the Herd

the consumption of DDT-infected lizards began killing the cats. As the cats disappeared, the rat population exploded. Although malaria was no longer a huge problem for the humans in the region, thanks to the rats, there was now plenty of typhus and plague to go around.

In order to restore ecological balance to the area, the World Health Organization determined that the best course of action would be to air-drop 14,000 live cats into Borneo via parachute. Before long, the mosquito population prospered once again.

L. A. Olsen never set out to become famous. His only plan that fateful afternoon in 1945 was to fetch supper, as his wife had asked him to do. Despite his years of experience in the art of chicken killing, he accidentally botched the decapitation of the fowl the world would soon come to know as "Mike, the Headless Chicken."

Olsen had managed to sever Mike's head just above the brain stem. Mike ran around the yard, as chickens normally do under these circumstances, but never stopped. Enough of the brain stem was still attached to what was left of the bird, which, as it turns out, is all a chicken needs to continue living. Olsen didn't have the heart to finish him off, so for the next eighteen months, he fed Mike with an eyedropper through the hole in his esophagus. The two went on the road in pursuit of fame and fortune. Spectators all over the country happily paid Olsen a few nickels for the privilege of seeing a real, live headless chicken.

Mike's unbelievable good luck eventually ran out. He died tragically in 1947. He choked on a kernel of corn that was too big for the hole in his neck.

Mary Kay Gray of Cheshire, Oregon, shot her husband in the back in 2006 when she discovered that he had killed her favorite chicken. Stanley Gray had blasted her chicken to kingdom come with a .44-caliber handgun, so Mary Kay shot him with her rifle. The violence escalated. When authorities arrived, the yard was littered with dead chickens. A neighbor told police that the Grays had only lived in the house next door for a month or so, and often appeared intoxicated. Stanley survived the assault. The chicken was pronounced dead at the scene.

It is said that Pond Square in London is haunted by the ghost of the chicken that was killed by Sir Francis Bacon in the seventeenth century. The English philosopher, statesman, and essayist had been riding in an open-air carriage through the snowy streets of London with his friend Dr. Witherborne, debating whether cold could be used to preserve meat as effectively as salt. In a spur-of-the moment decision to conduct the experiment right then and there, Sir Francis jumped out of the carriage and bought a hen from a local woman. The bird was killed, and Sir Francis immediately proceeded to stuff it with snow. Bacon died of pneumonia before confirming whether the experiment was a success, but many people in the centuries since have reported hearing a strange screeching in the middle of the night and the ghostly apparitions of a frantic chicken in Pond Square.

In 1999, a member of the Montana State House of Representatives was mauled to death by a cow. Elmer Severson suffered spinal cord injuries as a result of the scuffle. It is unclear whether Severson provoked the attack.

A Jack Russell terrier belonging to Andrew Turner, a Member of Parliament for the Isle of Wight, was held responsible for the murder of a polecat at a 2006 county fair. The terrier savagely shook the cat in its jaws, letting go only after someone threw a bucket of cold water on it.

Greek philosopher Chrysippus is believed to have died of laughter in 207 BC after watching his drunken donkey attempt to eat figs.

In 1834, Scottish botanist David Douglas fell into a concealed pit trap in Hawaii. He might have survived the fall, but was crushed to death by the wild bull that fell into the pit right after him.

There are many theories surrounding the death of the author Edgar Allan Poe, including that he died either of alcoholism, epilepsy, a diabetic coma, brain fever, or as a result of a beating from a band of thugs. He was found in a state of delirium outside a Baltimore tavern wearing tattered clothing that didn't belong to him. He died the following morning, on October 7, 1849, in a Washington, D.C., hospital. Based on a modern-day analysis of his state and the symptoms noted in his medical records, the most likely cause of Poe's death is that he was bitten by a wild animal and died of rabies.

Paul Nash of Ratcliff, Texas, struck a deer on Highway 7. Not sure whether the deer was dead, the distraught man quickly got out of his truck and went to render aid. Just then, another car coming from the opposite direction hit the deer again. Nash was impaled by the deer's antlers, killing him and whatever might have been left of the deer.

Timothy McKevitt and Jonathan Porter set out to exact revenge on an ostrich in Redwood City, California. The men had been trespassing on a ranch on Halloween night in 2006 when they were attacked by the giant bird. The men returned with guns and shot the bird dead. They were later charged with animal cruelty and felony possession of a firearm.

In 2006, a year-old coyote who would soon become known as "Hal" made his way safely from the wooded regions north of New York

City, through the Bronx and Harlem, and finally settled in Manhattan's Central Park. Despite having scared a few tourists and local residents, Hal did quite well for himself for several days. Animal control experts and others trying to catch him got a run for their money, but eventually did capture him. Authorities determined that the best thing for Hal would be to return him to nature. They transported him back to the wilds of affluent Westchester County, where he died of a heart attack in transit.

Quito the Gorilla finally bested his archenemy, Ben the Gorilla, at their home in the Jacksonville Zoo in Florida in 2006. During the last of their many bitter altercations, Quito chased Ben around the rocky tropical pit they were forced to share. Ben lost his footing on a slope, fell into the moat, and drowned. Zookeepers long suspected that the two were having relationship problems when, several weeks before, Quito bit Ben on the leg.

Winkie, a 40-year-old female Asian elephant that resided at a sanctuary in rural Tennessee in 2006, was believed to have been suffering a post-traumatic stress disorder flashback when she smacked her handler with her trunk and then stepped on her. The handler died instantly. Lewis County sheriff Dwayne Kilpatrick commented, "I had a friend of mine that got killed by a cow once."

Villagers in Jakarta found two human hands, a leg, skull fragments, some hair, and a pair of shorts inside a 16-foot, half-ton crocodile in 2006. In accordance with local religious beliefs, they hacked the crocodile to pieces and ate it. This ritual is believed to prevent other crocodiles from eating any more villagers.

A group of Turkish aviation technicians sacrificed a camel on the tarmac of Istanbul's Atatürk International Airport in December 2006, in celebration of having finally gotten rid of the last of a series of problematic planes. The aircraft had been leased to Turkish Airlines by Britain, and their frequent breakdowns caused all manner of consternation to the technicians over a period of thirteen years. Turks traditionally sacrifice animals as thanks to God when their wishes come true.

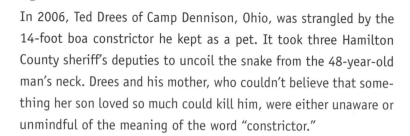

In 2006, Ted Drees of Camp Dennison, Ohio, was strangled by the 14-foot boa constrictor he kept as a pet. It took three Hamilton County sheriff's deputies to uncoil the snake from the 48-year-old man's neck. Drees and his mother, who couldn't believe that something her son loved so much could kill him, were either unaware or unmindful of the meaning of the word "constrictor."

In January 2007, William Coursey of Fayetteville, Georgia, shot a half-ton wild hog running loose in his neighborhood, then hung it from a tree in his front yard. This may have been one of four such hogs suspected of destroying the manicured lawns of that suburban area over a period of several years. No one was sure if the hog was unusually large or just average sized. "We don't keep records on hogs," said a representative from the Department of Natural Resources.

Beverly Lanouette of Enfield, Connecticut, was attacked by a large raccoon while she sat on her porch. The animal came up from behind and latched onto her leg, angry and growling. Lanouette beat the raccoon with a chair until it let go of her leg. Both Lanouette and the animal tested positive for rabies. Only Lanouette survived the 2007 incident.

Franklyn Pigott Jr. from Cape Coral, Florida, had tried everything to keep the bees off his property. In a last-ditch attempt, he mixed a product called Real Kill Indoor Fogger with the lubricant WD-40, and sprayed it on a nest of bees. The spray can turned into a flamethrower and destroyed the bees. It also set fire to Pigott's house.

A possum ran across a power line near a New Zealand ski resort in 2007, electrocuting itself and bursting into flames. It took firefighters twelve hours to put out the kilometer wide area of the mountainside that caught fire when the flaming animal fell to the ground.

A rampaging cow escaped from its field and ran amok in Chertsey, England. On the advice of the RSPCA, Chief Inspector Chris Moon and several highly trained firearms officers tracked the half-ton heifer and shot her dead after she charged at several residents in the vicinity.

Fisherman Ian Card was ecstatic when he hooked an 800-pound, 14-foot blue marlin off the coast of Bermuda during a 2006 fishing tournament. The swordfish leapt into the boat, stabbed Card in the chest with its 3-foot razor-like snout, and pulled Card into the water with the hook still in its mouth. Card survived the attack. The fate of the marlin is unknown.

After eighteen years, Salim Khan finally received $13,500 from the Jaipur District of India as compensation for the 1988 vehicular homicide of his elephant. Babli, the 35-year-old pachyderm, had been Khan's only source of income. The Rajasthan High Court of Jaipur ruled that Babli was "a living being," as opposed to "a livestock." Khan told the press that he would use the money to buy a new elephant and go back to the business of giving elephant rides to tourists.

Thinning the Herd

A 23-foot-long python invaded a fruit orchard in Malaysia and ate eleven guard dogs over a period of several days in 2007. Villagers finally caught the enormous snake and tied it to a tree, where it remained until wildlife officials arrived to take it away.

In 2002, a 61-year-old man ended his own life by climbing over a 3-foot wall in a Portugal zoo and taunting the lions. Most of the lions in the pit ignored him for a while, but when a 10-year-old lioness had had enough of the man's shenanigans, she walked over to him and broke his neck.

Yachtsman Graham Dalton was sailing near the waters of South Island, New Zealand, when he noticed a strange tangle of seaweed up ahead. He was too close and moving too fast to be able to change course in time, so his boat plowed right over it. Dalton heard a loud bump on the hull, immediately followed by a thud from the starboard rudder. When he looked back, he realized the seaweed had, only moments ago, been a seal.

A Michigan fisherman was attacked by an enraged 200-pound deer in 2001. David Gutowski was fishing quietly at the edge of a river when the animal charged him and tried to impale him with its antlers. Gutowski grabbed hold of the rack, wrapped his legs around the deer's rib cage, and hung on for nearly forty-five minutes. Gutowski finally managed to strangle the animal with his belt, and then clubbed it to death with a piece of wood. When wildlife officials told Gutowski that he could not take the dead deer home, he argued vehemently that he had earned the right to keep the deer. He had, after all, fought it and won, fair and square.

Birds in Redding, California, are particularly fond of the berry bushes that line Interstate 5. In the early spring of 2001, the berries began fermenting on the branches. Hundreds of inebriated birds began swooping down and flying erratically, crashing into windshields and dive-bombing into the pavement. No humans were reported hurt, but that area of the highway was littered with the avian victims of the alcoholic binge.

Mocha the Labrador retriever was not the first dog to succumb to the irresistible lure of a hot spring at Yellowstone Park. In 2001, she bolted toward the bubbling pool the moment her family opened the doors of their motor home. Mocha realized her mistake as soon as she hit the 200°F water. Despite the brave rescue attempts of her heartbroken owner, Donald Hansen, Mocha didn't make it.

Accidental dog boiling occurs with alarming regularity at Yellowstone Park.

The oldest known living creature, Harriet the Tortoise, passed away at the ripe old age of 176 in an Australian zoo. Harriet was reputed to have been found on the Galapagos Islands in 1835 by none other than the father of evolutionary science, Charles Darwin. When he found her, she was estimated to be about 5 years old and was no bigger than a Frisbee. Darwin originally named her Harry, not realizing for several years that Harry was a girl.

In May 2006, Gabor Komlosy was dragged into the Szamos River in Hungary by a 150-pound catfish. The 53-year-old man's body was later found still clutching his fishing rod, despite the fact that he had bashed his head into a rock and had either drowned as a result, or his lungs had taken in water after he was dead. The catfish was no less obstinate than its would-be assassin; its mouth was still clamped firmly to the other end of the fishing line.

A 6-year-old girl playing with a Pomeranian and a Jack Russell terrier in the backyard of their home was visited by a neighbor's pit bull. The intruder squeezed through a flimsy fence separating the properties, and immediately pounced on the two smaller animals, completely ignoring the little girl. Her father shot the pit bull twice in the neck, but it was too busy mauling the other dogs to notice. The Pom died of its injuries. The Jack Russell survived after extensive surgery. The pit bull was perfectly fine, even with two bullets still lodged in its neck.

In 1961, Murderous Mary, a 5-ton elephant with the Sparks Brothers Circus, reached over her handler to pick up a bit of watermelon on the side of the road. The handler used a hook to pull her back, catching her on a sore ear. Mary knocked the handler down and stomped his head flat.

A shark caught in 1967 in the waters near Cheviot Beach in Australia was cut open and found empty. Rescuers were looking for Prime Minister Harold Holt, who had disappeared when he went for a swim.

In the early days of space exploration, many animals were used as crash-test dummies before any humans were actually hurtled into outer space. Albert I was a rhesus monkey launched in a rocket by the United States in 1948. He reached an altitude of 39 miles, and suffocated during the flight. A year later, Albert II went up. This monkey actually survived the flight, but died on impact when his parachute failed. In 1959, after experimenting with many other primates, dogs, mice, and fruit flies, a squirrel monkey named Gordo reached an altitude of 600 miles in a Jupiter rocket. Monitoring equipment on board indicated that Gordo's respiration and pulse were unaffected by the great speed or distance he reached, proving that humans could, indeed, survive space travel. However,

NASA still had a few minor kinks to work out. Gordo's capsule sank to the bottom of the Atlantic Ocean on splashdown.

For all his careful and respected study of giant bears over a period of twenty-five years, Russian scientist Vitaly Nikolayenko learned the hard way that pepper spray doesn't work very well as a repellent on North American grizzlies. His bloodied and mangled body was discovered in 2003, inside a one-room hut in a desolate region near the Tikhaya River. Next to him were a giant paw print and an empty can of mace.

That same year, a self-proclaimed conservationist and documentary filmmaker named Timothy Treadwell met a similar fate. While compiling film footage on the wild bears in Alaska, and despite his claims that he had been accepted by "the clan" over the thirteen years he had been visiting the bears, parts of Treadwell and his girlfriend were discovered strewn throughout their camp. They were very small parts.

Walter Kopinger was considered one of the best hunters in his hometown of Ketzerbachtal, Germany, and so was the logical choice for taking care of business when a deranged pig broke into the laundry room of a neighbor's home in 2007. Kopinger assessed the situation, and chose a .357 Magnum over his regular hunting rifle, given the small dimensions of the room and the size of the pig. He blew the washing machine to bits, demolished the dryer, and destroyed a wall before finally hitting the unlucky porker, which later died of its injuries.

For more than 100 years, the labels on Tisbury Beer have contained the disclaimer, "This bottle is guaranteed monkey proof." The original head brewer at the English facility had a pet monkey that drowned in a vat of beer.

Sierra Stiles, an 8-year-old third-grader from Maryland, landed the first kill of the 2005 bear hunting season. The little girl shot a 211-pound bear twice in the chest with her rifle. "They won't eat now," Sierra said of the bears. "They won't eat a thing."

CHAPTER

11

JUST PLAIN
WEIRD

WHEN I DIE, I'D LIKE TO BE SCATTERED OVER MY HOMETOWN.
BUT NOT, LIKE, CREMATED OR ANYTHING.
Mitch Berg

SOME PEOPLE LIVE extraordinary lives—colorful, brilliant, awe-inspiring, fabulously exotic, adventure-filled lives. And then they die perfectly boring deaths.

None of them are in this chapter.

239

Kyujiro Kanaoka of Japan was registered as Itami City's oldest living resident. Too bad he had been dead for ten years. His sons, all of whom were in their seventies, believed their father was just resting. They had left him more or less undisturbed on his futon for more than a decade. When authorities discovered the decomposed body of the elder Kanaoka in 2005, one of the sons told them that he had recently consulted a relative, suspecting something might be wrong with their father.

In 1852, James "Yankee Jim" Robinson decided to become a pirate. The first thing he needed was a big boat. There were many of them docked off the coast of San Diego, so he took one. Yankee Jim was caught in the act, tried by a kangaroo court, and found guilty by a drunken judge. A makeshift gallows was hastily set up for the would-be pirate's execution.

Yankee Jim was very tall. The scaffold, alas, was not. He hung from the noose with his feet touching the ground, cursing and sputtering for nearly an hour. Lots of people watched. Eventually, he died.

Three years later, a man named Thomas Whaley built a house directly over the spot where he had watched Yankee Jim more or less dangle to death. Not long after, a little girl playing with Whaley's daughter in the backyard ran into a clothesline and strangled on the cord. That same daughter died at age 11 after ingesting a poisonous powder. Whaley's 17-month-old son died of scarlet fever. Another Whaley daughter, Violet, locked herself in the outhouse one day and shot herself in the head. Violet's death was ruled a suicide although no gun was found at the time. The weapon turned up many years later, buried under the concrete foundation of one of the exterior buildings on the property.

For the past hundred years, many people have reported sightings of the ghosts of Yankee Jim, the entire Whaley family, and even the Whaley dog. In the early 1960s, the U.S. Department of Commerce certified the Whaley family home as an official haunted house.

"John Doe of the Brooklyn Badlands" was the name given to the bits and pieces of a man who was murdered and scattered throughout New York in the summer of 2005. The first part of him to turn up was his bloody naked torso. It rolled down a conveyor belt at a paper recycling plant, much to the horror of Luis Landi, who, as fate would have it, was working the graveyard shift that night. Four days later, a volunteer at a Bedford-Stuyvesant church noticed flies buzzing around a trash bag. Inside was John's head. The rest of him was never found.

Pete Price, the host of the British radio talk show *Magic 1548,* became concerned when a frequent caller and terribly verbose "Terry from Liverpool" suddenly fell silent during a January 2006 broadcast. Price asked any listeners who might know Terry to find out what happened and render aid. Neighbors found Terry dead of a heart attack in his chair, with the phone still in his hand.

An elderly man from Adelaide, Australia, returned home from a short vacation and found a naked dead man in his bathroom. The 20-year-old intruder had broken into the man's home and helped himself to some prescription pills. The drugs turned out to be diabetes medication.

French prosecutors in the city of Rouen revealed that cannibalism was the most likely reason that some of the organs were missing from a dead prisoner. The suspected killer was a cellmate of the formerly intact convict. Under questioning, the suspect claimed to have eaten the victim's heart. What he ate, in fact, was part of the man's lung.

Al Mulock was a bit player in a series of cowboy movies and other productions in the United States and Europe during the 1950s and 1960s. He jumped to his death from his hotel window during the filming of Sergio Leone's low-budget *Once Upon a Time in the West*. Screenwriter Mickey Knox and production manager Claudio Mancini, who were working on a lower floor of the same hotel, saw Mulock's body fly past their window. They retrieved him from the street and took him to the hospital, where he died of his injuries.

When they returned to the set, Leone ordered Mancini to go back to the hospital and retrieve the costume; Mulock was still wearing it when he jumped.

Former drug addict, thief, and regular all-around hoodlum Ravindra Kantrulu converted to Islam in 2006 and began murdering homosexuals. His wife, Anjali, boarded a train and traveled many miles with their youngest child in tow. She went to the police station in Raipur, India, to attest to her husband's innocence. Anjali claimed that the bloodied shirt and ax the police found in Ravindra's possession when they arrested him must have been planted there by corrupt officials. Also, she explained, her husband couldn't stand the sight of blood. Although Ravindra had already confessed to killing at least fifteen of the twenty-one victims, Anjali argued, "He was very normal with me."

A Portuguese man wrote his last will and testament when he was 29 years old. In it, he designated seventy beneficiaries, all of whom had been selected at random from the Lisbon telephone book. He passed away in 2007 at the age of 42, leaving the heirs he had never met approximately $11,000 each.

Despite the government's claims of bumper crops in the region surrounding Maharashtra, India, distraught farmers have been killing themselves at a rate of about a hundred per month since the mid-1990s. The mass suicides began after switching to the government-approved, genetically engineered Bollgard cotton seeds, which seem to produce nothing but failure in that part of the world. The government continues to insist that the seeds are good.

The pilot of a 2006 Continental Airlines flight bound for Puerto Vallarta, Mexico, from Houston, Texas, told his crew he wasn't feeling well shortly after takeoff, and then dropped dead. The copilot made an emergency landing at another Texas airport. The plane continued to its destination with a new crew. The airline happily reported that passengers were only slightly inconvenienced.

The men who buried Attila the Hun and his treasures in AD 453 were put to death immediately upon their return so that the feared barbarian's grave would never be discovered.

American volcanologist David A. Johnston was reporting on the 1980 eruption of Mount St. Helens in Washington State. Even if he had been standing several miles away, it still would have been too close. His last words were heard over a two-way radio: "Vancouver, Vancouver, this is it!"

Issei Sagawa, who was a student in Paris in 1981, invited a beautiful Dutch classmate, Renée Hartevelt, to his home for dinner. Shortly after she arrived, Sagawa killed her. Then he ate her.

In January 1919, a 30-foot "wall of goo" swept through Boston, killing 21 people and injuring 150 others. Unseasonably warm temperatures caused a giant tank filled with molasses to burst open and spew two million gallons of the sticky substance all over the center of the city. The massive wave destroyed buildings, swallowed up horses, and swept away wagons and everything else in its path. Rescue efforts were nearly impossible; rescuers were either carried away in the thick wave or became hopelessly stuck in the syrup.

Duane Allman and Berry Oakley of the famed Allman Brothers Band both died in eerily similar traffic accidents. Duane was killed in a motorcycle crash in October 1971 in Macon, Georgia. One year and one month later, Berry Oakley also died in a motorcycle accident in the same city.

A small cedar chest containing the ashes of a 95-year-old woman disappeared from its niche in a Houston mausoleum in 2005. The woman's daughters made the horrifying discovery when they went to visit their parents' final resting place, and found a can of sour cream and onion potato chips where their mother's cremains should have been.

According to her husband, 31-year-old Elisabeth Otto had been feeling a bit homesick for her native Germany in recent months. While on a chartered commuter plane traveling from Roseville to San Jose, California, in December 2000, Elisabeth opened the cabin's emergency exit door and jumped out in mid-flight. She landed with a splat in a community vegetable garden in Sacramento.

Irv Rubin, a militant leader of the Jewish Defense League, was imprisoned no fewer than forty times throughout his career as an advocate for his cause. His last arrest, in 2002, was on charges that he was plotting to blow up a mosque. While in prison, police reported that Rubin slashed his own throat with his razor, then jumped 15 feet from a balcony.

Rubin was declared dead several times over the next ten days. One report stated that he had died during surgery. Another said that he was brain-dead and soon to be pulled from life support. The final report was that he was really dead. Mrs. Rubin claimed all this as proof that her husband was murdered by a hit man hired by the federal government.

A pig farmer from Vancouver became Canada's deadliest serial killer in 2007. Willie Pickton murdered and dismembered forty-nine women in his slaughterhouse. He told an undercover police officer that he wanted to kill one more, to bring the total to a nice even fifty.

In September 2006, a group of masked men in military garb burst into the *Sol y Sombra* bar in Mexico and tossed five human heads into a crowd of dancers. Beheadings have become rather commonplace throughout Mexico in recent years, as a way of intimidating police and exacting vengeance on rival drug dealers and other enemies.

Two British women were killed by a giant inflatable maze shaped like a castle in Riverside Park in England in the summer of 2006. The attraction, known as Dreamscape, covered an area roughly equal to half a football field. It consisted of a series of rooms and tunnels made of rubberized panels filled with air. Approximately thirty people were inside when a gust of wind tore the installation from its moorings and sent it hurtling more than 100 feet into the air.

William Kogut was a death row inmate at San Quentin in the 1930s. Believing he could fashion an execution for himself that was less horrific than any the State had in store for him, Kogut unscrewed a hollow steel leg from his cot and packed it tightly with torn pieces of playing cards, which Kogut knew were printed with ink that contained a very volatile material. He poured water into the other end of the tube and placed the device between his head and the gas heater in his cell. As the heated water turned into steam, pressure built up in the tube. The ensuing explosion was powerful enough to blow a hole through Kogut's skull, in effect making him the first prisoner to execute himself using a pipe bomb, and perhaps the only person ever to blow his brains out with a deck of playing cards.

In 2006, 27-year-old Jason Chellow of rural Placer County, California, was killed by his own house. Although the house was built in the 1980s, no one knew that it had been constructed over a long-defunct mine. As Jason entered the kitchen, a giant hole opened up and sucked him underground. It took rescuers several days to extract the man's body from the cave-in.

The toasty-warm skeleton of a 40-year-old woman was found in her small London studio apartment in January 2006. Joyce Vincent was on the floor surrounded by Christmas presents, lying between a space heater and the television set. Both appliances were still running. Police believed she had been dead for three years. She was discovered by housing association officials who had come to collect thousands of dollars in overdue rent.

❧

A U.S. World War II bomber plane named *Lady Be Good* crash-landed in the desert in Libya in 1943. Sixteen years later, oil surveyors from Britain stumbled on the wreckage that had been extraordinarily well preserved by the dry climate. The machine guns, radio, and one of the engines still worked, and there were several containers of fresh water on board. There was, however, no sign of the nine crew members who had been on this flight.

The Air Force did not take the sighting seriously when it was first reported by the oil surveyors. It would be another year before they sent a search team to the site. In 1960, the wreckage and the mummified remains of eight of the nine crew members were finally located.

Parts of *Lady Be Good* are still on display at the Army Quartermaster Museum in Fort Lee, Virginia. Through the years, night watchmen have reported hearing voices and eerie sounds near the display, and that pieces of the plane often move by themselves.

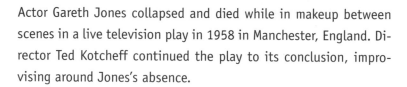

Actor Gareth Jones collapsed and died while in makeup between scenes in a live television play in 1958 in Manchester, England. Director Ted Kotcheff continued the play to its conclusion, improvising around Jones's absence.

Mabelle Clark's grandson, Ernest, moved into her tiny public housing apartment in Newark, New Jersey, when the boy's mother went to jail for murdering her abusive prizefighter husband. Strange things began to happen in 1961, the year Ernest turned thirteen. Objects began hurling themselves through the apartment. Dishes were smashed and visitors were pelted with whatever was handy by some unseen force. Mabelle didn't want to tell anyone of these phenomenal events because she feared losing her apartment. Neighbors complained of the noise, however, and the Housing Authority stepped in to investigate. They witnessed the poltergeist activity firsthand, yet concluded that it had to have been the troubled boy who was causing it.

It was later revealed that the disturbances began about two weeks before Ernest's mother escaped from prison, and ended a few weeks after she was captured and sent back to jail. Ernest had been removed from the home and was gone for at least two weeks before the supernatural activity finally ended.

Thinning the Herd

Actor Paul Mantz was a flying prodigy in the early twentieth century. He came out of retirement in 1965 to work as a stunt pilot in *Flight of the Phoenix,* the story of crash survivors who attempt to construct a new aircraft from pieces of the wreckage. Mantz successfully landed the pieced-together airplane during the first test run. While filming the second attempt, the plane failed to clear a sand dune. Mantz was decapitated when the engine broke away.

William Bullock was killed in 1867 by his own invention, the web rotary press. A driving belt came off its pulley, so Bullock kicked the machine to get it going again. The press swallowed his leg and then proceeded to mangle it. The leg became gangrenous within a few days. Bullock died during the amputation procedure intended to save his life.

Radio broadcaster and *New York Times* critic Alexander Woollcott was alternately described as "witty and genial" and "bombastic and gossipy," usually by the same people. His affectations and overblown personality made him an easy target, as evidenced during a radio hoax involving a deathbed plea from two elderly spinsters. The women begged Woollcott to recite the Twenty-third Psalm to them on the air. Woollcott served up a rousing rendition, replete with accompaniment by the CBS Radio Orchestra, and wept openly when told that the fake old ladies had passed away.

Woollcott himself suffered a fatal heart attack while on the air in 1943, during a particularly heated discussion on Adolf Hitler. Listeners to the radio broadcast noticed that Woollcott seemed strangely silent during much of the show. He had died at some point in the middle of the broadcast.

Massachusetts inmate Michelle Kosilek, who was Robert Kosilek when he went to prison, petitioned the federal courts to have the government pay for the final steps in his sex-change surgery. Kosilek said that being trapped in a man's body was like "the dying I do inside a little bit every day." Kosilek's wife, on the other hand, did all her dying at once. He had strangled her to death with a piano wire in 1990.

Thinning the Herd

Certain Christian sects incorporate snake handling into their religious services. Believers in this practice state that no harm will come to a snake handler who is "right with God."

In the spring of 2006, the reverend Dwayne Long of Jonesville, Virginia, incorporated a snake-handling segment into his church's Easter Sunday service. He was killed by the venomous rattlesnake. When church members later were asked whether they thought Reverend Long was not "right with God," they explained, "It was just his time to go."

The *Michelin Guide* rates the best restaurants in France using a system of stars; a 3-star rating indicates the very best of the best. Chef Bernard Loiseau was very proud of his restaurant's hard-won 3 star Michelin rating. In 2003, however, another restaurant publication, the *GaultMillau,* downgraded chef Loiseau's rating from 19 to 17 on their own review scale. Loiseau was beside himself, distraught over the possibility that this review might cause him to lose one of his Michelin stars, making his restaurant merely "very, very good." He put a shotgun to his head and blew his brains out.

As a helicopter touring the Grand Canyon was returning to its base at the end of its sightseeing run, Timothy Clam suddenly unfastened his seat belt and jumped out, plunging 4,000 feet to his death. No one knows why.

Detective Allan Pinkerton, considered America's first great detective, tripped on a sidewalk in 1884 and bit off a bit of his tongue. He died of the ensuing infection.

Ignoring warnings about a bridge being out due to roadwork, Tom Mix, star of many 1940s cowboy films, crashed his 1937 Cord into a gully. The accident itself was minor, but it dislodged an aluminum suitcase from the backseat of his car, which smacked him in the back of the head and killed him. Interestingly, Mix's faithful horse, Tony Sr., died on the same day exactly two years later.

Thinning the Herd

Leslie Harvey, guitarist of Stone the Crows, was electrocuted on-stage during a concert in Wales in 1972. The plug on the microphone was not grounded. Unfortunately, Harvey was.

A truck driver identified only as "Martin T." suffocated to death under 16,000 pounds of manure. The 34-year-old man was in the process of dumping the load in a field near the western Czech city of Karlovy Vary.

Melinda Duckett killed herself with a shotgun blast to the head after being interviewed a little too harshly by the famously vitriolic television news show host Nancy Grace. In a lawsuit filed against CNN and Nancy Grace, the family alleged that the host's questions weren't about finding Duckett's son at all, as promised, but about accusing the woman on television of murdering the boy herself.

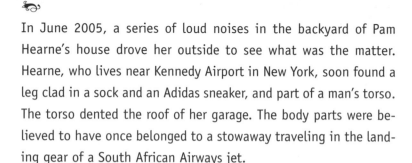

In June 2005, a series of loud noises in the backyard of Pam Hearne's house drove her outside to see what was the matter. Hearne, who lives near Kennedy Airport in New York, soon found a leg clad in a sock and an Adidas sneaker, and part of a man's torso. The torso dented the roof of her garage. The body parts were believed to have once belonged to a stowaway traveling in the landing gear of a South African Airways jet.

Russian cosmonaut Yuri Gagarin was the first man in space and one of his country's greatest heroes. During a training exercise on the new MiG-15UTI rocket in 1968, Gagarin crashed just outside of Moscow. They found his body hours later, frozen and reeking of alcohol.

While delivering the New York City helicopter traffic report in her usual witty style, WNBC-AM radio listeners heard Jane Domacker scream, "Hit the water! Hit the water!" Some listeners actually saw the chopper plummet into the Hudson River that day in 1986.

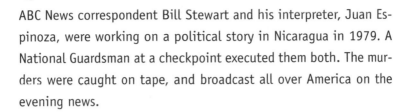

ABC News correspondent Bill Stewart and his interpreter, Juan Espinoza, were working on a political story in Nicaragua in 1979. A National Guardsman at a checkpoint executed them both. The murders were caught on tape, and broadcast all over America on the evening news.

Pizza deliveryman Brian Wells was as dependable as he was predictable. His daily routine was invariable, and he had never been in trouble with the law. In 2003, while standing outside the bank he had just robbed, he told police officers surrounding him that he had been kidnapped by three people and coerced into committing this crime. A simple pipe bomb was elaborately locked around his neck. Wells begged police to let him go because the kidnappers had set the bomb to go off minutes after the well-planned robbery. While they waited for the bomb squad to arrive, the device exploded, instantly killing Wells.

Brandon Vedas lived quietly at home with his mother in Arizona. The 21-year-old's social circle consisted mostly of friends with whom he visited daily via webcam on the Internet. While drinking rum and smoking pot one evening in 2003, his chat-room buddies encouraged him to keep popping tranquilizers and other pills he had handy. Vedas's mother found him the next afternoon. She had not noticed anything out of the ordinary, and had spent the previous evening doing crossword puzzles in the next room.

A Greek family on vacation quickly canceled their holiday plans shortly after arriving at their hotel room. The father walked over to one of the beds to inspect a strange lump under the covers, which turned out to be a severed human head.

In case you missed it, the "secret" behind Victoria's Secret was that Victoria was a man named Roy Raymond. The other interesting thing about Roy Raymond was that he jumped to his death from the Golden Gate Bridge in 1993.

In July of 1966, an 18-year-old crewman named John Pedder lost his life during a routine water-tight drill on board the *Queen Mary*. He was crushed to death while trying to slip under Door 13 as the hatchway was closing.

The families of British tourists Andrew Redfern and Louis Selo—who had never met and whose sons died under completely different circumstances in two different countries—faced a strangely similar problem. Andrew died in October 2006 after falling on his forehead in a hotel lobby in Cuba. Louis died of a heart attack one month earlier, while vacationing in Dublin, Ireland. Andrew was returned to England without his lungs, kidneys, and part of his brain. Louis was sent back with two hearts and four lungs. The families are still waiting for a believable explanation.

Absurdist playwright Alfred Jarry of France was the inventor of *Pataphysique*, the science of imaginary solutions. He often wandered the streets of Paris under a bright green umbrella, wearing cycling gear and two guns, and speaking in the high falsetto voice of one of his characters. He died at the age of 34 in 1907, the net result of alcoholism and tuberculosis. His last words were, "I am dying. Please, bring me a toothpick."

DEATHS FORETOLD

THE FUTURE WILL BE BETTER TOMORROW.

—J. Danforth Quayle,

former Vice President of the

United States of America

I AM OCCASIONALLY plagued by the suspicion that some of the people who have been locked up in psychiatric facilities or who hear voices that others do not, may in fact be more evolved than we know, attuned to some wavelength the rest of us have never learned to access. Maybe we lock them up because we're jealous of the fact that no one occupies the empty rooms in our own heads, and if they do, they don't find us interesting enough to talk to. Maybe we give those people pills to shut them up because we want to do all the talking.

Or maybe they really are nuts.

But even the sanest among us (if, in fact, there are such people) occasionally have "a funny feeling," an experience, or some powerful blast of recognition whose origins we couldn't begin to explain. And then, afterward, we try to put a rational spin on it. "It was like déjà vu, but different," we say, as if that made perfect sense. Or we say, "What a lucky coincidence that I decided to get off the train one stop before it derailed!" without mentioning that our actual destination was still miles away.

I'm glad for the fact that, at least in some respects, I'm not so adamantly skeptical or hopelessly cynical as to require an ironclad explanation for every seemingly unnatural event. There is a certain poetic beauty in knowing that life still holds some mysteries. A rational explanation for everything might make it all much too ordinary, too sad, bereft of magic. I like being filled with wonder from time to time, even if it is a fleeting delusion.

Bernadette Soubirous was a poor French girl who saw a vision of the Virgin Mary at a grotto in Lourdes. Her body was exhumed several times in the decades following her death and was found to be incorruptible—a term that describes a corpse that shows no signs of decomposition long after it should have turned to dust. The Catholic Church considers the incorruptibility of a corpse to be one of the signs of sainthood.

At the site of Bernadette's vision, The Lady instructed the young girl to dig into the dry, barren earth with her bare hands. A spring of fresh water miraculously emerged. Countless millions have visited the grotto since 1862, with many reporting recoveries from devastating illnesses and injuries after drinking or touching water from the spring.

Despite having contracted a painfully debilitating bone disease some years later, Bernadette was informed by The Lady that the water would never heal her, so she never sought relief for her own suffering at the grotto.

Bernadette died at the age of 35 at the Convent of Nevers. Her body was exhumed in 1909, thirty years after her death, and found to be incorruptible. Her clothing was damp and she was sprinkled with sawdust from the rotting casket, but the corpse itself was intact, and actually emitted a sweet fragrance.

Bernadette was exhumed and reexamined in 1919, and then again in 1925. Except for a darkening of her skin that might have occurred during the first exhumation when nuns bathed and re-dressed her, there was hardly a change in the condition of her corpse. She was finally placed in a crystal coffin in a chapel at the Convent of Nevers. Her body has been on view ever since, and can still be seen bearing the remarkable appearance of fresh youth.

In 1914, John Howlet, a Newfoundland sealer, told his wife of a chilling nightmare in which he was on a mountain of ice, terri-fied, lost, and freezing, surrounded by vague, indefinable "things." Two weeks later, Howlet was among 120 sealers aban-doned on an ice floe in the North Atlantic after a horrific ship-wreck. The missing men were not discovered for two days, by which time more than half the men were dead. Howlet was one of the lucky few who survived.

In 1898, fourteen years before the *Titanic* disaster, author Morgan Robertson published the novel *Futility*. The novel was about a ship named *Titan*. It was nearly the same size as *Titanic* and carried al-most the same number of passengers. Each ship, the real one and the fictitious one, struck an iceberg in the North Atlantic in mid-

Thinning the Herd

April and sank, with the loss of over half of their passengers due to insufficient lifeboats.

Another author, W. T. Stead, also wrote numerous stories and articles predicting that a large ocean liner would sink with the loss of over half on board due to the lack of sufficient lifeboats. Stead, an avid believer that the ghosts of the dead roamed among the living, received three separate warnings that travel would be dangerous in the month of April 1912. One such warning came from a very live person, a clergyman who wrote to Stead predicting a catastrophe on water. Despite these warnings, Stead booked passage on the *Titanic* and died in the disaster.

Several of the *Titanic*'s staff and crew either failed to show up, resigned their posts, or ignored premonitions of disaster—their own or those of their loved ones. Some were just the happy beneficiaries of dumb luck.

- Second Engineer Colin MacDonald turned down the offer to join the crew of the *Titanic* because of a "gut feeling" that something was going to go wrong.

- Crewman Bertrand Slade missed his train and arrived after *Titanic* had set sail.

- Chief Officer Henry Tingle Wilde was originally scheduled for the White Star Line's ship, the *Olympic*. Despite tremendous misgivings, he joined *Titanic*'s crew at the request of Captain Smith. The day before she sank, *Titanic* was docked at a port of call in Queenstown, Ireland. Wilde used the opportunity to write a letter to his sister. He told her, "I still don't like this ship. I have a queer feeling about it." Wilde perished in the disaster.

- Luigi Gatta, manager of the controller's office for *Titanic*, dismissed his wife's comments about "feeling strange" about the ship's maiden voyage.

- John Morgan, owner of the ship, became suddenly ill and was unable to sail.

Others who missed the launch or canceled at the last minute include the following:

- Millionaire George Vanderbilt canceled his plans the night before the trip, claiming a longtime superstitious fear of being on a ship's maiden voyage. It was, in fact, his mother-in-law who had sent an urgent telegram begging him to change his plans. Vanderbilt's luggage was on board when the ship sank.

- Robert Bacon, U.S. ambassador to Paris, claimed "last-minute business" and canceled his trip.

- Frank Adelman and his wife sailed on a later ship after Mrs. Adelman convinced her husband that they must not travel on *Titanic*.

- A scheduled passenger identified in official reports as Mr. Shepherd received a frantic telegram from his wife, begging him to travel on a different ship. He did.

- Henry Frick canceled his trip after his wife sprained her ankle. It wasn't a serious injury, but it served as a convenient and believable excuse for changing their minds so soon before sailing.

- Horace Harding changed his plans for reasons he couldn't quite explain and rebooked his trip on the *Mauritania*.

- James O'Brien canceled because he had witnessed a robbery and was ordered to testify in court in Ireland.

- Edward Bill's wife was yet another one of many spouses who begged their husbands not to travel on this ship. He heeded the warning and survived.

A woman scheduled to board a transatlantic passenger ship became inexplicably queasy and anxious the moment she laid eyes on the luxury liner. The day before launch, the ship's mascot, a small black cat, ran away and was never seen again; several crewmen were heard to remark that this was a particularly bad omen. Another passenger who had booked passage on the ship, a successful shoe dealer from Boston, canceled his passage the day before the trip, finding himself unaccountably concerned and frightened. The ship was the *Lusitania*, sunk during World War I by a German torpedo in May of 1915. Nearly 1,200 people lost their lives in that tragedy.

David Booth had a vivid and recurring dream ten nights in a row. He dreamt of an American Airlines flight taking off on a sunny day, its nose pointing straight up but making a noise that didn't seem right. The plane suddenly banked to one side, dived toward the ground, and exploded in an enormous ball of fire. Each time, David awoke from this dream full of overwhelming despair.

Plagued by the notion that he should do something about this and knowing he might be dismissed as just another kook, David nonetheless contacted the FAA and recounted his dream to an official over the phone. Without details regarding a specific place and time, there was nothing anyone could do.

On the morning of May 25, 1979, David awoke with the certainty that he would never have this dream again. It was on that very day that American Airlines flight 191 crashed in a field near the runway at O'Hare Airport shortly after takeoff. The incident happened in a manner the thirty-year FAA official who had spoken to David Booth would later describe as "eerily accurate."

A flight attendant scheduled to fly on Eastern Airlines flight 401 had a strong premonition of danger and refused to go as scheduled. She also managed to convince her crew not to take that flight. That plane crashed into the Florida Everglades in 1972, killing 101 of the 172 passengers and crew on board.

Shortly before Sunna Roulston set off on the vacation of a lifetime in Asia, she had an extremely disturbing dream in which she found herself wandering amid crowds of strangers, cold and wet, lost in a jungle. People everywhere were bruised and battered. The scene was one of total chaos.

Unwilling to change her plans because of one silly dream, she nonetheless felt compelled to write a good-bye letter to her family.

Deaths Foretold

Sunna told a friend that if anything should happen while she was away, the friend should look for the envelope she left on her bedside table.

While sitting in a longboat in the waters off the coast of Thailand, Sunna Roulston witnessed the giant tidal wave that killed more than 8,500 people and injured 4,500 others in the December 2004 tsunami disaster.

Three separate and independent organizations began to study an unusually high number of reported premonitions and prescient dreams from all over the United Kingdom in 1966. London psychiatrist J. C. Parker compiled and analyzed the compelling data. This experience led him to create the British Premonitions Bureau, which still exists today. The bureau has been unable to prevent any disasters, but has had some success in predicting several of them.

The events leading up to the creation of the bureau involved a terrible disaster in a small Welsh village. The mother of a 10-year-old boy awoke one night from a chilling nightmare in which her son went to school, but the building was buried under something black. Another woman from the same town reported a similar dream, in which she found herself suffocating in blackness. Several others recounted dreams of small children or a school being buried by a large landslide. One man in a distant northwestern town in England, who had no connection whatsoever to the people or events in Wales, claimed that he had a dream that consisted only of letters being spelled out in dazzling white lights: ABERFAN.

On October 21, 1966, in Aberfan, Wales, 116 children and 28 adults were killed when a large mountain of coal collapsed. The black avalanche buried a small section of the town, including an elementary school filled with children.

The tristate area near the shared borders of Missouri, Oklahoma, and Kansas is known as the Spooksville Triangle. Almost every night for the past hundred fifty years, a strange ball of light can be seen bouncing along a road known as Devil's Promenade. As it moves, it leaves behind a trail of luminous sparks. Many scientists have studied this phenomenon but have never been able to agree on an explanation. Residents of the area refer to the light as The Devil's Jack-o'-Lantern.

Actor Richard Lawson, star of the soap opera *All My Children,* had a bad feeling about USAir flight 405. He had had no fewer than four close brushes with death in his life. On that snowy night in March of 1992, as he sat strapped into his seat on the plane already on the runway, he was overcome with a very strong premonition that he was about to experience a fifth encounter with the Reaper.

A last-minute seating change may have been the only thing that saved his life. The plane went down shortly after takeoff from LaGuardia Airport in New York. More than half of the passengers died in the frigid waters of Flushing Bay. Lawson was able to swim out of the submerged plane and out through a nearby hole in the wreckage.

Kendra St. Charles-Hall was another passenger on the plane. She changed seats twice before the plane took off. She survived the crash, but the people who took her previously assigned seats did not.

For months before his death, country music singer Johnny Horton was haunted by ominous premonitions that he would be killed by a drunk. While waiting to perform at the Skyline Club in Texas in November 1960, he became nearly hysterical when bandmates suggested they hang out at the bar. He hid far away from the bar, certain his killer was waiting for him there. After the show, the band loaded their gear into Horton's Cadillac, and he headed home to

Shreveport, Louisiana, wanting nothing more than to put Texas behind him. On the way, a truck crashed into Horton's Cadillac on a bridge in Milano, Texas, killing the singer. The driver of the truck was charged with intoxication manslaughter.

The eerie coincidences of Horton's life did not end there. His last gig was at the Skyline Club, exactly where his friend, Hank Williams, had performed his last show. Williams also died in a car accident after that performance. Horton became close with his widow, Billie Jean, and married her the following year. Billie Jean became a musician's widow twice, having lost both husbands in the same way after having performed at the same club.

HMM

ALWAYS GO TO OTHER PEOPLE'S FUNERALS.
OTHERWISE, THEY WON'T COME TO YOURS.

—Yogi Berra

*ONCE YOU'VE SEEN Britney Spears emerge from a limo without even
her usual tiny slingshot of a panty to cover what's left of her dignity,
you realize one important thing: Death is the only real taboo left in
this country.*

*We don't like to talk about it. We don't like other people talking
about it. We make up euphemisms for it so we don't have to say the*

D-word: going to greener pastures, meeting our maker, making our transition, getting fitted for a toe tag, napping in the freezer. We say to our loved ones, "If I die . . ." as if that were only one of many possible outcomes. In America, denial equals immortality.

I would never suggest that we shouldn't be afraid to die. The tragedy, really, is that we are too often afraid to live.

A Gallup poll revealed that 32 percent of Americans believe in ghosts. Even more believe that haunted houses really do exist. About 88 percent of all Americans believe in heaven, but only 71 percent believe in hell. Despite acknowledging the inevitability of death, nearly all Americans express "shock" and "disbelief" when someone they know dies.

There was a time when the nuclear family consisted of parents, children, grandparents, cousins, aunts, and uncles, all living under the same roof, or in very close proximity. If you grew up in a family, you saw nearly everyone die at home and in bed, with friends and relatives gathered around. Few Americans these days die at home, or are present at the time of a loved one's passing.

Consequently, funeral homes are relatively new to the American way of death. Many cities and states have banned the practice of holding a wake in a family's home. In the old days, however, people simply cleared the kitchen table and set up the recently departed in a coffin with the lid propped open. This was done for two reasons: so that friends and neighbors would have a chance to pay their last respects, and, more importantly, to wait a day or two to make sure the dearly departed was really dead; premature burials were a fairly common occurrence in those days.

The custom of covering the face of a dead person with a sheet evolved from an ancient pagan ritual. People believed that a person's spirit escapes through the mouth at the time of death. In an effort to keep the spirit inside the body and possibly delay death, they would hold the dying person's mouth and nose shut. This surely finished off more pagans than whatever disease was killing them.

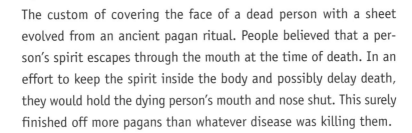

Every society in the world has its own way of caring for the dead, but humans throughout history and in every part of the world have always incorporated these three things:

- some type of ritual or ceremony

- a revered place for the disposition of the body

- memorialization of the dead

Even Neanderthal man, who walked the Earth more than 60,000 years ago, had a special way of dealing with life's aftermath. Prehistoric burial grounds have been found with human remains that were laid to rest with carefully arranged animal bones and flowers. It appears to be encoded in our nature to respect and honor the dead.

Some of us, however, sometimes choose to ignore that instinct.

Morticians and owners of American funeral homes earn frequent-flier miles every time they ship a corpse.

Casket companies in the United States have had to start building extra-large coffins in response to the "super-sizing" of America.

As of the end of 2006, nearly two hundred people have been "buried" in outer space. Through an agreement with NASA, commercial service organizations can arrange for a small sample of a deceased person's cremains to be launched into space during an already-scheduled space shuttle mission. The ashes are placed in a container about the size of a lipstick tube, and then released while the rocket is orbiting the Earth, the moon, or even as far away as Pluto. In the cheap version of the service, the tubes eventually return to Earth through the planet's gravitational pull, then burn up and disintegrate during reentry.

Some famous persons buried in space include Gene Roddenberry (*Star Trek* creator), Timothy Leary (hippie and philosopher), James Doohan ("Scotty" from *Star Trek*), and Leroy Gordon Cooper Jr. (one of the original Mercury Seven astronauts).

Hmm

Elephant graveyards have long been a part of the mythology of the animal kingdom. While elephants do not actually dig holes and bury their dead as humans do, they certainly exhibit clear signs of distress when they come upon the remains of one of their own.

Only a few other animals besides humans and elephants show any interest in their dead. Chimpanzees experience prolonged periods of grief, distress, and strange behavior in the presence of a dead social-mate or relative. They abandon the body only when it begins to decompose. A lion, on the other hand, may sniff or lick at a dead lion, and then eat it.

Lions are not the biggest threat to humans wandering the jungles of Africa. Hippos kill many times more people than any other wild mammal on that continent.

Thinning the Herd

The female European cuckoo bird never makes her own nest. She lays all of her eggs in the nests of other species of birds. The poor bird that finds itself involuntarily pushed into the role of "foster mother" may recognize the strange egg and abandon the nest, but more often she shows compassion for the abandoned chick, incubating and hatching the cuckoo egg along with her own. Shortly after emerging from its shell, the baby cuckoo instinctively shoves all the other eggs and young birds over the edge of the nest, forcing the foster parents to care only for the cuckoo. The consequences can prove especially tragic if the foster parents are tiny compared to the large baby cuckoo. They work themselves nearly to death to find enough food to satisfy the hunger of the freakish creature they think they have produced.

Eagles make their nests at great heights, in mountains or treetops. The first baby eaglet to hatch will push all of its siblings out of the nest as they come out of their eggs. In this manner, all of the food the mother eagle brings will be only for the one that hatches first.

Hmm

Sharks are voracious killers almost from the moment they are conceived. The largest shark fetus developing in its mother's womb will devour its smaller brothers and sisters so it won't have to share any of its food. Shark fetuses will also feed on the mother's steady supply of unfertilized eggs.

In any given year, fifteen times as many people are killed by falling coconuts than by sharks.

On average, about twelve people die each year in Britain as a result of violent altercations with vending machines.

A person will die from total lack of sleep sooner than from starvation.

Skinny people who do not exercise are twice as likely to die prematurely than obese people who stay active.

At least nineteen people have been boiled to death in Yellowstone National Park since it opened in 1872. Many others have been seriously injured in the park's many hot springs. The overwhelming majority of these visitors jumped into the steaming pools trying to rescue their overly enthusiastic and not-too-bright dogs. Bear attacks and suicides also occur quite regularly at the park.

Throughout history, humans have considered suicide so abhorrent and frightening that nearly every culture has developed special ways of disposing of the corpses or ritualizing these deaths. In the eighteenth century, the English impaled the corpses with a stake and buried the bodies at a crossroads to confuse those unquiet spirits and keep them from coming back to life as vampires. In other European countries, the corpses of suicides were either set on fire, dragged through the streets, thrown in garbage heaps, or put in a barrel and dumped in a river.

Some of the most popular suicide spots in the world are:

- The Golden Gate Bridge in San Francisco

- The Grand Canyon of Verdon in southeastern France

- The Gap, a cliff face in Sydney, Australia

- The Space Needle in Seattle, Washington

- The Eiffel Tower in Paris, France

- Dealey Plaza in Dallas, Texas, where President Kennedy was assassinated

- The Hollywood sign in Los Angeles, California

- Yellowstone National Park, which covers parts of Wyoming, Montana, and Idaho

The Japanese are perhaps the only culture that regards suicide as an honorable way to resolve particularly embarrassing predicaments. About 30,000 people kill themselves each year in Japan. Despite the deeply ingrained mores of tradition and the apparent lack of horror over such an act (at least as compared to other nations and cultures), there have been calls to ban certain best-selling books that glorify the subject or provide how-to information. A thriller written by Seichi Matsumoto in the late 1990s idealized Mount Fuji as the perfect suicide spot. The year the book was published, seventy bodies were found in or around the dormant volcano.

Since its opening in 1937, San Francisco's Golden Gate Bridge is by far the most popular suicide spot in the world. On average, one person takes a leap from the bridge every two weeks. Of the more than one thousand jumpers, fewer than thirty have lived to tell of the experience. Almost all of the survivors reported changing their minds the second they let go of the railing.

Over the years, the Golden Gate has earned the nickname "Bridge of Sighs." After a walk across the bridge, many people have spoken about the eerie sensation that the bridge was whispering to them. Friends and family members of people who have jumped often speak of being utterly perplexed by their loved one's decision to jump, claiming he or she didn't seem suicidal at all before deciding to take a walk along the bridge.

Interestingly, no one has ever jumped from the San Francisco Bay Bridge, which is just a couple of miles away, spans the waters between San Francisco and Oakland, California, and is clearly visible from the Golden Gate Bridge. Perhaps the reason has something to do with the fact that it is very ugly, especially compared to the mesmerizing beauty of the legendary Bridge of Sighs.

The beautiful Grand Canyon of Verdon in the lush southeastern region of France attracts more than a million visitors a year. Some of them never leave. The Canyon is as popular a suicide spot as San Francisco's Golden Gate Bridge. Since the building of barriers along the road in the 1980s, fewer people have been able to jump into the canyon or drive their cars off the cliffs, but they are finding it just as easy to take a leap off the nearby Artuby Bridge.

Women attempt suicide three times more often than men, but men actually succeed at killing themselves three times more often than women. Poets and writers commit suicide much more frequently than anyone else, at the astounding rate of twenty times the national average. Artists are somewhat less disturbed, killing themselves only ten times more frequently. A person is three times more likely to commit suicide if he or she is a medical doctor. Dentists, police officers, and lawyers also figure prominently on the high-risk scale.

Suicide rates increase dramatically under right-wing conservative governments. A recent study found that 35,000 more suicides occurred in Great Britain over the past 100 years whenever the Tories were in power. The British government declined to comment on the findings.

Florida has one of the highest rates of execution of prisoners in the United States, but it occasionally runs into a sticky little dilemma. The preferred method of execution is by lethal injection, but it cannot be performed by doctors for ethical reasons. Executioners occasionally botch the process because they have no medical training.

Fortunately, Florida death-row inmates can opt for the alternate choice: Old Sparky. No medical training required.

Myanmar has one of the world's strictest laws against the use of narcotics. Drug users can be punished by death for indulging in certain substances. In October 2000, that country's military junta declared caffeine to be a narcotic.

Hmm

In ancient China, women sometimes drank mercury heated in oil to deal with the pesky little problem of unwanted pregnancies. The potion was 100 percent effective in aborting fetuses, and more than 98 percent successful in killing the mothers.

On average, New York City recycling plants and trash-processing facilities find at least one dead body (or portion thereof) about every eighteen months.

Number of confirmed deaths in America caused by contaminated Halloween candy given to children by strangers: 0

Number of confirmed deaths caused by contaminated Halloween candy given to children by their own relatives: 1

Every year, *Forbes* magazine publishes a list of the world's richest dead celebrities. These were the Lucky 13 for 2006:

Kurt Cobain	$50 million
Elvis Presley	$42 million
Charles M. Schulz	$35 million
John Lennon	$24 million
Albert Einstein	$20 million
Andy Warhol	$19 million
Dr. Seuss	$10 million
Ray Charles	$10 million
Marilyn Monroe	$8 million
Johnny Cash	$8 million
J. R. R. Tolkien	$7 million
George Harrison	$7 million
Bob Marley	$7 million

Hmm

Sources

EVERY EFFORT WAS made to authenticate the veracity of these stories. The overwhelming majority were checked against three or more legitimate news and reference sources, such as Associated Press, Reuters, Encyclopaedia Britannica, and other similarly respected outlets. The very few that had only one or two verifiable references came directly from local newspaper accounts, academic or government reports, and encyclopedic or literary publications.

Some of the funniest and most interesting stories I found were originally posted on a variety of popular Internet sites. Unfortunately, they were not all true, accurate, or verifiable. I only included the ones that could be legitimately validated.

AAP General News (Australia)

ABC News

AboutVienna.org

Adoption.com

A&E Television Networks

Aerospaceweb.org

The Age (Melbourne, Australia, newspaper)

Alberta Report (Canada)

All Headline News

All Philosophy.com

American Experience (PBS)

American Transcendentalism Web (a biography of Henry David Thoreau in an online article by Ann Woodlief, Virginia Commonwealth University)

Amsterdam News (New York)

Ananova (UK)

Anecdotage.com

Answers.com

The Antioch Review

The Arab American News

Archive Photos.com

Arkansas Tonight (Online Radio and Politics)

Art Hazards News

Asbury Park Press (North Carolina)

Associated Press

Atlanta Journal-Constitution

Atlantis Rising magazine

The Australian (national newspaper)

Aviation History magazine

AZCentral.com (Arizona)

Bartleby's Quotes (Bartleby.com)

BBC News

Beliefnet.com

Belleville News-Democrat (Illinois)

Benjamin Franklin: A Biography by Ronald W. Clarke (2004)

The Best, Worst & Most Unusual by Bruce Felton and Mark Fowler (1994)

Billboard magazine

Biography Channel

The Birmingham Mail (England)

The Birmingham Post (England)

The Book of Scotland by William Chambers (1830)

Books and Writers (www.kirjasto.sci.fi)

Boston City Guide

The Boston Globe

Boston Herald

The Brussels Journal (Belgian newspaper)

Busca Biografías.com

Canadian Encyclopedia.com

Captain Cook Country (www.captaincook.org.uk)

The Catholic Encyclopedia

Catholic Pilgrims.com

CBS News

CDC (Centers for Disease Control)

Celebrate Today.com

Celestis Space Services of America

Central Jersey *Home News Tribune*

CFW Enterprises.com

Channel 4 News (Jacksonville, Florida)

Channel 6 ABC News (Philadelphia)

ChicagoArtistsResource.org

Chicago Sun-Times

Chicago Tribune

China Daily (newspaper)

ChinaUnix.net

The Christian Century

The Cincinnati Post

Civil War Home.com

Classics at MIT

Clear Path International News

CNN

Columbia Encyclopedia

The Concise Oxford Dictionary of Quotations

Coney Island Museum

Cosmopolitan magazine

Court TV Crime Library

The Cromwell Association

Crosscurrents magazine

Cuisine du Monde

The Daily Breeze (Los Angeles)

The Daily Herald (Illinois)

The Daily Mail (London)

The Daily Mirror (London)

The Daily News (Los Angeles)

The Daily Post (Liverpool)

The Daily Press (Victorville, California)

The Daily Record (Glasgow, Scotland)

The Daily Telegraph (London)

Dave's Daily.com

Dead Musicians Directory

Death Penalty Information Center

De Telegraaf (Dutch newspaper)

Deutsche Presse-Agentur (German Press Agency)

The Dick Cavett Show

Discovery Channel

Dorset *Daily Echo*

Dutch News Service (Netherlands)

Dynamic Chiropractic newsletter

Early American Literature magazine

Earthview.com

Ebony magazine

The Economist

eHistory.com

8Notes.com

The 11th Armored Division Association

Encyclopaedia Britannica

Encyclopedia Americana (Grolier's)

ESPN

Esquire

The Evening Standard (London)

The Examiner (San Francisco)

Eyewitness to History.com

Fact Monster.com

Famous Last Words by Barnaby
Conrad (1961)

Fernbank Science Center (Atlanta, Georgia)

Find a Grave.com

Florida Museum of Natural History's International Shark Attack File

Folklore magazine

Forbes magazine

Fort Myers *News-Press*

Forward (New York newspaper)

Fox News (Australia)

Fox News (U.S.)

Gallup Poll

Gaudi Club (Barcelona)

Goodbye! magazine

Grizzly Man (documentary film)

Grove Concise Dictionary of Music

The Guardian (UK)

The Handbook of Texas Online

Harper's Magazine

The Heinz Family Philanthropies, 1994 Heinz Awards speech by Teresa Heinz

Helena *Independent Record*

The Hindu (India)

Hinduism Today magazine

History of Funeral Customs by Wyoming Funeral Directors Association

A History of the Roman World from AD 138 to 337 by H. M. D. Parker (London, 1958)

History Wired (Smithsonian Institution)

Houston Chronicle

The Humanist magazine

Humanities magazine

The Human Marvels.com

IMDB (Internet Movie Database)

The Independent (London)

Independent News & Media

The Independent on Sunday (London)

India Abroad.com

InfoPlease.com

Insight on the News

Interavia Business & Technology

International Cemetery and Funeral Association

International Herald Tribune

Ireland's Eye.com

The Journal (Newcastle, England)

The Journal of Criminal Law and Criminology

Journal of Neurosurgery

KHNL Channel 8 News (Hawaii)

Knight Ridder / Tribune

Knot magazine

Kyodo World News Service

The Last Days of Socrates by Plato (1993)

The Last Link on Left.com

Las Vegas Review-Journal

Lawlink (New South Wales Public Defender's Office)

Legacy Matters (www.estatevaults.com)

Lettres de Madame de Savigné (April 26, 1671)

Lewis Center for Educational Research

Lexington Herald-Leader (Kentucky)

Life magazine

Lincoln Journal Star (Nebraska)

The Literature Network

Liverpool Daily Post (UK)

Liverpool Echo (UK)

The Lives and Opinions of Eminent Philosophers by Diogenes Laertius (2006)

Lives of the Noble Greeks and Romans by Plutarch (AD 75)

Local London Network

London Free Press (Ontario, Canada)

Longview *News-Journal* (Texas)

Los Angeles Times

The Magazine Antiques

The Mail on Sunday (London)

Mammoth Cave National Park (official website)

Mark Twain A–Z by Kent Rasmussen (1996)

Messenger-Inquirer (Owensboro, Kentucky)

Miller Center of Public Affairs, University of Virginia

Milwaukee Journal Sentinel

The Mirror (London)

Mosaic (Winnipeg)

Most Haunted (Travel Channel television series)

MSNBC News Services

My Heart Is My Own by John Guy (2004)

NASA History Division

The Nashville News (Arkansas newspaper)

The Nation

National Catholic Reporter

The National Directory of Haunted Places by Dennis William Hauck (1994)

National Geographic

The National Park Service

National Parks magazine

National Review magazine

NBC News

New Music Classics.com

New Scientist

New Statesman magazine (UK)

New Straits Times

New York *Daily News*

New York Post

The New York Times

The New Zealand Herald

News Channel 3 (California)

The News Letter (Belfast, Northern Ireland)

News-Record (Piedmont Triad, North Carolina)

News24.com (South Africa)

Newsweek

Niagara Falls Daredevil Museum

North County Times (California)

Noticias Locas (Argentina)

November of the Soul: The Enigma of Suicide by George Howe Colt (2006)

NPR (National Public Radio)

The Oakland Tribune (California)

Ohio History Central Online Encyclopedia

Onstage magazine

Oops! by Paul Kirchner (1996)

Orkneyjar.com (Heritage of the Orkney Islands)

Orlando Sentinel (Florida)

The Oxford Dictionary of Byzantium

Oxford Student Publications

The Palm Beach Post (Florida)

PBS

The Pennsylvania Gazette

The People (London newspaper)

The Philadelphia Inquirer

Political Graveyard.com

Pope-Pourri by John Dollison (1994)

Proceso magazine (Madrid)

Psychology Journal

Quadrant magazine

Realm of St. Stephen: A History of Medieval Hungary by Pal Engel et al. (2001)

Real Premonitions (A&E television documentary)

Reason magazine

The Record (Bergen County, New Jersey)

ReefQuest Centre for Shark Research

The Register-Guard (Eugene, Oregon)

Reuters

The Review of Contemporary Fiction

Roadside America.com

Rocky Mountain News (Denver)

Rolling Stone magazine

The Sacramento Bee

The St. Petersburg Times (Florida newspaper)

Salidas de Emergencia by Eduardo Allende (2006)

Salon.com

The San Diego Union-Tribune

San Diego Zoo "Animal Bytes"

San Francisco Chronicle

Scandinavian Studies magazine

Schott's Original Miscellany by Ben Schott (2003)

The Scotsman

Seattle Post-Intelligencer

The Seattle Times

The Sir Walter Raleigh Collection

Skeptical Inquirer magazine

SkyNews magazine

The Smoking Gun.com

Snopes.com

South Florida Sun-Sentinel

SouthPole.com

South Wales Echo (Cardiff)

Spiegel Online International News Service

The Star-Tribune (Minneapolis)

The Straight Dope.com

Studies in English Literature, 1500–1900 by David Stymeist (2004)

Stunt Players.com

Suddenly Senior.com

The Sun (UK)

The Sunday Mail (Glasgow, Scotland)

The Sunday Mercury (Birmingham, England)

The Sunday Mirror (London)

Swannanoa Valley Museum

The Swindon Advertiser (UK)

The Taipei Times

The Telegraph (India)

Texas Escapes Online Magazine

TexasScapes.com

Texas State Library and Archives Commission

Time magazine

The Times (Sydney, Australia)

The Times of India

The Times-Mirror (Los Angeles)

Times-News (Burlington, North Carolina)

Today in Science History (todayinsci.com)

Trivia-Library.com

TV.com

TVNZ (New Zealand)

The 20th Century by David Wallechinsky (1995)

Undiscovered Scotland

United Press International

University of Delaware

USA Today

U.S. News & World Report

Vanity Fair magazine

Virginia Military Institute Archives

The Virginian-Pilot

The Wall Street Journal

Warsaw Times-Union (Indiana)

The Washington Post

The Washington Times

The Wave magazine

The Weekly Standard

The Western Mail (Cardiff, Wales)

The White House Online History Page

White Star Line Ships (official website)

Who Was Frank Silvera? by Garland Lee Thompson (online article at www.fsww.org/whois.html)

Wiltshire Times & Chippenham News (UK)

Windsor Star (Canada)

The Women's Review of Books

Worldwide Gourmet.com

WSB-TV News (Atlanta)

Wyoming Funeral Directors Association

Yellowstone National Park (official website)